MW00777902

Law, Literature, and Violence Against Women

This book engages legal and literary texts in order to examine acquaintance crimes, such as rape, sexual harassment, stalking, and domestic abuse, and to challenge how the victim's physical or psychological "freeze response" is commonly and inaccurately mistaken for her consent.

Following increased interest in the #MeToo movement and the discoveries of sexual abuse by numerous public figures, this book analyzes themes in law and literature that discredit victims and protect wrongdoers. Interpreting a present-day novel alongside legislation and written court cases, each chapter pairs a fictional text with a nonfictional counterpart. In these pairings, the themes, events, and arguments of each are carefully unpacked and compared against one another. As the cross-readings unfold, we learn that a victim does not "ask for it," and she should not arouse suspicions just because she does not fight, run away, or report the crime. Instead, and as this book demonstrates, the more common and most practical response is to become physically and mentally paralyzed by fear; the victim dissociates, shuts down, and remains stuck in the fright and captivity of abuse.

This book will interest scholars and students working in, and especially at the intersection of, law, literature, gender studies, and criminology.

Erin L. Kelley is Professor of English at Dallas College, USA.

Law, Literature, and Violence Against Women

Ending the Victim Blame Game

Erin L. Kelley

a GlassHouse Book

First published 2025
by Routledge
4 Park Square, Milton Park, Abingdon, Oxon OX14 4RN

and by Routledge
605 Third Avenue, New York, NY 10158

Routledge is an imprint of the Taylor & Francis Group, an informa business

a GlassHouse book

British Library Cataloguing-in-Publication Data
A catalogue record for this book is available from the British Library

Library of Congress Cataloging-in-Publication Data
Names: Kelley, Erin L., 1973- author.
Title: Law, literature, and violence against women: ending the victim blame game / Erin L. Kelley.
Description: Abingdon, Oxon [UK]; New York, NY: Routledge, 2024. | Includes bibliographical references and index.
Identifiers: LCCN 2024015428 (print) | LCCN 2024015429 (ebook) | ISBN 9781032301341 (hardback) | ISBN 9781032301389 (paperback) | ISBN 9781003303572 (ebook)
Subjects: LCSH: Women–Violence against–Law and legislation. | Women–Crimes against–Law and legislation. | Sexual harassment of women–Law and legislation. | Sexual abuse victims–Legal status, laws, etc.
Classification: LCC K5191.W65 K45 2024 (print) | LCC K5191.W65 (ebook) | DDC 345/.05046082–dc23/eng/20240409
LC record available at https://lccn.loc.gov/2024015428
LC ebook record available at https://lccn.loc.gov/2024015429

ISBN: 9781032301341 (hbk)
ISBN: 9781032301389 (pbk)
ISBN: 9781003303572 (ebk)

DOI: 10.4324/9781003303572

Typeset in Times New Roman
by Deanta Global Publishing Services, Chennai, India

To every survivor who finds a piece of themselves within these chapters. I believe you, and I support you.

Contents

1 Introduction

Law, Literature, Gender-Based Violence, and a Culture of Disbelief

Interpersonal Violence, Gender, and Power

We know that violence does not discriminate, and it is a global issue that affects every demographic. However, statistics show that female-identifying victims are disproportionately impacted in crimes that involve interpersonal violence.[1] Unlike "stranger violence," interpersonal violence occurs between people who are acquainted with one another, and a power differential within the pair leverages one person's controlling influence over the other. Interpersonal violence consists of physical, sexual, verbal, emotional, or financial abuse, and the perpetrator may also stalk, threaten, or blame the victim.[2] Romantic couples within heterosexual, LGBTQ+, and gender non-conforming communities are subject to interpersonal violence. It may occur not only between romantic couples, but also amongst bosses and employees, parents and children, friends, classmates, and co-workers.

In this book, I cover specific types of interpersonal, gender-based violence in heterosexual couples—husbands and wives, current or past romantic partners, and bosses and employees. I define this type of violence as gender-based violence because although some exceptions exist, decades' worth of studies have indicated that in these couplings, those who identify as women are

1 Sylvia Walby and Jude Towers, *Measuring Violence to End Violence: Mainstreaming Gender,* 1 Journal of Gender Based Violence, 1, 1 (2017). See also *Invisible Women: The Forgotten Victims of Gender-Based Violence,* Podcast on Crimes Against Women, (June 5, 2023) (downloaded using ITunes). This podcast states that "every nine seconds in this country a woman is assaulted by someone who told her that he loved her, by someone who told her it was her fault, by someone who tries to tell the rest of us it's none of our business … and [that] perpetrator [is] a liar."

2 Susan S. Ricci, *Violence Against Women: A Global Perspective*, 3.1 Women's Health Open Journal, 1, 1 (2017).

DOI: 10.4324/9781003303572-1

disproportionately impacted as victims.[3] I explain that the reason why most victims are women and why most perpetrators are men is because men's violence against women has become normalized.[4] Even more so, blame and the "weight of … responsibility" has been shifted from the male wrongdoer to the female victim.[5] Created by a system that favors patriarchy, this phenomena has "served to protect men's power and privilege and offer impunity for their infractions."[6] These men not only engage in physical, mental, and emotional harm, but also they impose "subordination [that] depriv[es] women of liberty, autonomy, dignity, and equality."[7] Gender-based violence, therefore, is both violence and discrimination.[8]

This book is the first to combine the fields of law, literature, neuroscience, and gender studies to examine forms of interpersonal, gender-based violence such as acquaintance rape, domestic abuse, stalking, and sexual harassment. By interpreting a present-day American novel alongside legislation and written court cases, each chapter pairs a fictional text with its nonfictional counterpart(s). In these pairings, the themes, events, and arguments of each are carefully unpacked and compared against one another. As the cross-readings unfold, we learn that a victim does not "ask for it," and she should not arouse suspicions just because she does not fight, run away, or report the crime. Instead, the more common and most practical response demonstrates that she becomes physically and mentally paralyzed by fear. As a result, she most often dissociates, shuts down, and remains stuck in the captivity of abuse and in a system that fails her, and her paralysis may be both acute and long-term. Through an interdisciplinary analysis, I reveal that a victim's physical or psychological "freeze response" is commonly and inaccurately mistaken for consent. I argue that by ignoring the brain's natural response to trauma,

3 Lynnemaire Sardinha et al., *Global, Regional, and National Prevalence Estimates of Physical or Sexual, or Both, Intimate Partner Violence Against Women in 2018*, The Lancet, 339.1037. (Feb. 16, 2022). https://www.thelancet.com/journals/lancet/article/PIIS0140-6736(21)02664-7/fulltext This global study found that from 2000 to 2018, one in four women had experienced domestic abuse. See also *The Quest for Justice: Improving Legal Representation for Survivors of Gender-Based Violence,* Podcast on Crimes Against Women (March 6, 2023) (downloaded using ITunes), which states that 90 percent of crimes against people who identify as women are committed by men.

4 *Id.* at *The Quest for Justice: Improving Legal Representation for Survivors of Gender-Based Violence.*

5 Michelle L. Meloy and Susan L. Miller, The Victimization of Women: Law, Policies, and Politics, 7 (2011).

6 *Id.*

7 Evan Stark, *Current Controversies: Coercive Control*, in Domestic Violence Law, 48 (Nancy K.D. Lemon, ed. 2018).

8 Kathy Humphries, *A Health Inequalities Perspective on Violence Against Women,* 15.2 Health and Social Care in the Community, 120, 120 (2007).

American law that has been historically influenced by a culture of disbelief unjustly blames the female victim for her abuse.

A Culture of Disbelief of Women

A major challenge that reinforces violence against women includes patriarchal "social conditioning—the way our systems of family life, education, employment, entertainment and pop culture, spirituality and religion … contribute to the unrelenting prevalence of sexual assault, domestic violence" and other forms of abuse.[9] In this book, I examine longstanding, commonly accepted, gender-biased social standards that have crossed over cultures, historical time periods, and geographical locations. Of course, not all people believe that men have the right to abuse women; however, I contend that this concept exists as the rationale behind the acceptance of men's violence against women, and it is the "norm" for the status quo. One belief that encourages violence includes the idea that women should remain submissive to men in the home and "that men have the right to discipline women for incorrect behavior."[10] Under this guise, domestic violence becomes acceptable. Other examples consist of the notion that women should not deny sex to their partners, that sexual harassment is "normal," and that women are most valued as wives and mothers and not as individuals.[11] In other words, women should exist by the discretion of masculine order, direction, and pleasure. Under this patriarchal belief system, men are valued over women solely due to their gender, and this contributes to a culture of disbelief that signifies men's authority—at any cost—over women.

To that end, I also argue that due to a predominant part of a culture that tends to devalue females, a woman who speaks out against her male abuser is automatically viewed through a lens of suspicion, and she is disbelieved for a variety of reasons. In sexual assault cases, widely accepted rape myths such as "she's lying," "she consented," or "she asked for it" due to her provocative clothing or her "promiscuity" shift blame to the victim and negate the crime. In domestic violence cases, "she's lying" or "her circumstances cannot be that bad since she stays with him" are common misconceptions that both discredit the victim and diminish the wrongdoing. Like both domestic violence and sexual assault cases, common beliefs such as "she's lying," "she asked for

9 Elizabeth Hamilton Guarino, *The Best Ever You Show Welcomes Joy Farrow and Laura Frombach* (Dec. 5, 2023) (downloaded using ITunes). https://www.besteveryou.com/post/the-best-ever-you-show-welcomes-joy-farrow-and-laura-frombach

10 OXFAM International, *Ten Harmful Beliefs That Perpetuate Violence Against Women and Girls,* OXFAM.org (Jan 1, 2023), https://www.oxfam.org/en/ten-harmful-beliefs-perpetuate-violence-against-women-and-girls. See also Manon Garcia, We Are Not Born Submissive: How Patriarchy Shapes Women's Lives (2021).

11 *Id.*

it," "she's exaggerating," or "she consented" dismiss the abuse in both stalking and sexual harassment cases. These knee-jerk, unsubstantiated reactions perpetuate ongoing fallacious, biased conclusions embodied by a culture of disbelief that reinforces violence against women.

United States Law, Consent, and the "Freeze" Response

Historically, the law does not recognize mental health or signs of trauma, especially in victims. In crimes against the state such as rape, domestic violence, and stalking, the prosecutor must prove every element of the crime beyond a reasonable doubt. In most states, one of the elements the prosecutor must prove includes a defendant's "guilty" state of mind—or mens rea—to show that he "knowingly" or "willfully" intended to harm the victim.[12] On the contrary, a defendant's mens rea is removed from a sexual harassment suit because sexual harassment is not a crime. Instead, it is a violation of Title VII of the Civil Rights Act and a civil dispute between two parties. The burden of proof—a preponderance of evidence standard—is lower than that of a criminal case. However, like rape, domestic violence, and stalking, sexual harassment victims consist of mostly women whose perpetrators are men.[13] In these cases, a victim plaintiff must prove that the defendant possessed the intent to abuse her physically or verbally in "a sexual nature, including lewd remarks, salacious looks, and unwelcome touching."[14] Like the other forms of violence, his intent is most often disproved due to an underlying assumption that the female victim somehow consented to his "advances." Thus, the defendant may successfully show that sexual harassment did not occur, and instead, she was a willing participant in the encounter between two consenting adults. However, I argue that what looks like a victim's "consent" in sexual harassment and the other forms of violence most often relates to a victim's innate, neurobiological freeze response—of the fight, flight, or freeze response to danger and trauma. This freeze response, which is typically unrecognized by US law, might look like acquiescence or consent when in fact it determines the opposite.

In this book, I examine both the acute freeze response that arises when the violence initially happens and the long-term freeze response that may occur when the victim either is unable to process their trauma or they are continually

12 *Mens Rea*, Black's Law Dictionary (11th ed. 2019).

13 In a study by the EEOC, women filed a disproportionate number of 78.2 percent of the sexual harassment charges between 2018 and 2021. USEEOC, *Integrated Mission System, Charge Data, FY 2018-2021*(Apr. 2022) https://www.eeoc.gov/data/sexual-harassment-our-nations workplaces#:~:text=Sexual%20harassment%20or%20sexual%20assault,been%20a%20top%20agency%20priority.

14 *Sexual Harassment*, Black's Law Dictionary (11th ed. 2019).

exposed to ongoing abuse. *Fight*, *flight*, and *freeze* are terms used to describe the way our brains tell our bodies how to react when we are exposed to real or perceived danger.[15] Also referred to as "tonic immobility," the freeze response is initiated when victims cannot fight or flee.[16] Instead, they may freeze by internalizing the abuse. When a victim is sexually assaulted or sexually harassed, they may describe feeling physically and mentally paralyzed and incapable of defending themselves.[17] The freeze response may look like giving in, acquiescing, or "consenting"; however, in fact, many victims describe feeling so shocked that they cannot move, speak, or think clearly.[18] Some might even psychologically disassociate.

I also argue that domestic violence and stalking victims may experience the acute freeze response when the abuse occurs. However, domestic violence, sexual harassment, and stalking crimes differentiate from sexual assault since these victims most often experience more than one incidence of violence. To that end, I examine the long-term, "functional freeze" response that can result in a psychological paralysis due to the repetitive nature of the abuse. I contend that domestic violence victims have adopted certain survival mechanisms due to Post-Traumatic Stress Disorder (PTSD) that conceal their distress to the outside world and help them endure their life behind closed doors.[19] In this sense, many victims have acquired coping mechanisms such as "learned helplessness," where they do not ultimately fight or flee their abuser—which is typically expected by both law and our contemporary culture.[20] Instead, they mentally "freeze" and learn to make do with the ongoing harm.[21] Similar to acquiescence or disassociation during a sexual assault, "many battered women become so demoralized and degraded by the fact that they cannot predict or control the violence that they sink into a state of psychological paralysis and become unable to take any action at all to improve or alter the situation."[22]

Like domestic violence victims, many stalking and sexual harassment victims acquire coping mechanisms such as "learned helplessness" where, in the end, they cannot or do not ultimately fight or flee their abuser. While victims

15 Norman M. Schmidt, et al., *Exploring Human Freeze Responses to a Threat Stressor*, 39.3 J Beh Ther Exp Psychiatry, 292, 292 (Sept. 2008).

16 *Id.* at xvii.

17 Jim Hopper, *Freezing During Sexual Assault and Harassment*, in Psychology Today (Apr. 3, 2018), https://www.psychologytoday.com/us/blog/sexual-assault-and-the-brain/201804/freezing-during-sexual-assault-and-harassment#:~:text=Freezing%20happens%20in%20many%20sexual,effects%20on%20experience%20and%20behavior.

18 *Id.*

19 Martha Chamallas, Introduction to Feminist Legal Theory, at 341 (Vol. 3 2013).

20 Claire Dalton and Elizabeth M. Schneider, *The Criminal Justice System* in Battered Women and the Law, 564, 575 (2001).

21 Dalton and Schneider affirm that "battered women tend to 'give up' in the course of being abused; they suffer psychological paralysis" (107).

22 State v. Kelly 97 N.J. 178; 478 A.2d 364, 371(1984).

may have initially tried to fight their stalker by reporting the crime, most victims do not acquire adequate assistance from law enforcement or support from the criminal justice system. Thus, they might have also attempted to flee by changing their contact information, by hiding, by staying with family or friends, by changing their appearance, or by moving to a new location in order to get away from the stalker.[23] After all attempts have been exhausted, victims often give up by learning to make do with the harm and live in intense fear that is sometimes described as "psychological terrorism."[24] This form of psychological terrorism and functional freeze may also be present in sexual harassment victims who experience ongoing abuse. The fact that they fear retaliation or loss of employment may also contribute to the trauma. Specifically in the chapter, I provide examples of symptoms of PTSD such as "re-experiencing, effortful avoidance, emotional numbing, and hyperarousal factors that victims might use as coping mechanisms for long-term abuse."[25]

DARVO

An acronym created by psychology professor Dr. Jennifer J. Freyd, DARVO stands for Deny, Attack, Reverse Victim and Offender.[26] DARVO is a form of manipulation that shifts blame from the perpetrator to the victim. It is a mechanism by which sexual offenders may avoid responsibility for their wrongdoing. In terms of gendered violence, DARVO relies on deeply embedded, harmful social attitudes that reinforce masculine aggression and superiority and feminine passivity and inferiority. DARVO can occur on both an individual and societal level. In this sense, I argue that DARVO is one of the reasons why so many female victims do not report the violence, and that when they do, oftentimes they are still not supported or believed. Understanding DARVO helps combat gendered violence.

The Divisiveness of Third-Wave Feminism

This book is designed to support women—all women. However, in my view, a divisiveness exists between third-wave feminists that separates and weakens

23 Neal Miller, *Stalking Investigation, Law, Public Policy, and Criminal Prosecution as a Problem Solver*, in Stalking Crimes and Victim Protection: Prevention, Intervention, Threat Assessment, and Case Management 401, 387 (Joseph A. Davis, ed., 2001).

24 Dalton and Schneider, at 575. See also Doris M. Hall, *The Victims of Stalking* in The Psychology of Stalking: Clinical and Forensic Perspectives 133, 113 (J. Reid Meloy, ed., 1998).

25 Patrick A. Palmieri and Louise F. Fitzgerald, *Confirmatory Factor Analysis of Post-Traumatic Stress Symptoms in Sexually Harassed Women*, Journal of Traumatic Stress, Dec. 28, 2005, 657, 657.

26 Jennifer J. Freyd, *Violations of Power, Adaptive Blindness, and Betrayal Trauma Theory*, 7 Feminism and Psychology, 22, 22 (1997).

us. Unlike the second generation, the third-wave legal feminists (from 1990 and beyond) recognize that women are a diverse group. While these feminists consider "complex identities," they are nonetheless separated into three subgroups: intersectional feminists, postmodern feminists, and autonomy feminists.[27] Nonetheless, in the name of diversity, these three camps tend to compete against one another, and each maintains their own strengths and limitations. Thus, in this third generation, "feminists have become used to the idea that they are likely to disagree."[28]

Intersectional legal feminists focus on intergroup dynamics by identifying distinct ways in which gender, race, and class overlap. According to Rafia Zakaria, white feminists like myself "refuse to consider the role that whiteness and the racial privilege attached to it have played and continue to pay in universalizing white feminist concerns, agendas, and beliefs as being those of all feminism and all feminists."[29] Contrary to this statement, I do not believe white women are the "experts" on feminism. I do not think that my experience as a white feminist supplants those of women of different races, ethnicities, statuses, and identities. In fact, by recognizing differences and challenges within the larger whole, intersectional feminists provide a unique voice for each minority group that must continue to be heard and recognized. They help us understand that "while the differences between men and women are significant, so are the differences among women."[30]

On the contrary, opponents of intersectional legal feminism argue that creating lines of division within a group weakens the feminist movement altogether. Separating different types of subjugation obscures the mutually reinforced discrimination among all women.[31] By isolating the minority groups, sometimes intersectional legal feminists make an inaccurate, sweeping generalization about the most privileged subgroup of white women.[32] Thus, they may falsely assume that a common form of discrimination between all women does not exist. This rationale proves counterproductive and can "tarnish feminist-inspired legal reforms, rendering them inadequate to meet the needs of large groups of women."[33]

27 Martha Chamallas, Introduction to Feminist Legal Theory 23 (3rd ed. 2013).
28 *Id.* at 24.
29 Rafia Zakaria, Against White Feminism ix (2021).
30 Mary Joe Frug, Postmodern Legal Feminism x (2000).
31 Chamallas at 24.
32 *Id.* at 27.
33 *Id.* at 29.

Postmodernist Legal Feminism

This book most closely aligns with intersectional legal feminism's "competitor," postmodern legal feminism. Unlike intersectional legal feminists who create categories, postmodern legal feminists concentrate on intragroup dynamics. They argue that all women have been constructed by a patriarchal view that historically creates the male/female binary.[34] As a result, this group examines socially constructed gender biases that filter into legal reasoning and serve to reinforce discrimination. Although intersectional feminists might argue that an evaluation based on a male/female binary proves reductive, American law in its creation and interpretation explicitly and implicitly applies this binary. Backed by statistics, the law has historically defined "victims" as females and "perpetrators" as men in violent crimes against women. Thus, postmodern legal feminists elucidate this distribution of patriarchal power within society and the law: "It is through women's sexual characteristics that men define women, and having defined them, [men] forcibly and *legally* subordinate them."[35] Ultimately, while intersectionalists might suggest the postmodern legal feminist approach is oversimplified, I would respectfully argue the same for intersectionalism: they might claim that I do not consider the "individual parts," and I claim that they do not consider the "whole." Notwithstanding, I do not negate the fact that intersectional legal feminists have positively contributed to both the scholarly and cultural discourse, and I commend, respect, and support their achievements. However, this book will examine the common ground of sexual discrimination that exists between all women, and this concept most closely aligns with the postmodern legal feminist perspective.

Analyzing Law as Literature

The hermeneutics of both law and literature discern value and meaning through critical analysis and close reading. For example, a judge establishes common law in written court opinion through narrative "facts" and legal elements, while a literary critic analyzes rhetoric and metaphor that reflect legal, political, historical, and/or cultural themes. By broadening the scope of legal analysis, scholars such as Ronald Dworkin suggest that law can also be read and analyzed as literature: "we can improve our understanding of law by comparing legal interpretation with interpretation … [of] literature."[36] Such practice reconnects law to the human condition within the legal framework that regulates it, and both literature and law may express shared knowledge

34 Maxine Eichner, *On Postmodernist Legal Theory*, 36.1 HARV. C.R.-C.L. L. REV. 1, 9 (2000).

35 CATHERINE MACKINNON, FEMINISM UNMODIFIED: DISCOURSES ON LIFE AND LAW 40 (1988).

36 Ronald Dworkin, *Law as Interpretation*, 9.1 CRITICAL INQUIRY,179, 179 (1982).

and distinctive values within a society. For example, Kieran Dolin explains that written court opinion may be interpreted as literature that reflects cultural attitudes and social practices.[37] Seeking a more comprehensive understanding of how law, language, and society interact, this approach reads legal decisions as "cultural texts."[38] Advancing Dolan's idea, this book adopts the method of selecting and reading US legal decisions and American novels as cultural texts that uncover discrimination against victims of violence against women. By analyzing these works together, I highlight the legal system's lack of support combined with a culture of disbelief, and I examine common misconceptions that shift blame to the victim. I demonstrate how the mistake of implicating the victim signifies a more complex situation than "she lied" or "she asked for it." Instead, I elucidate the powerlessness forced upon her by both the male perpetrator who attacks her and a system that fails her.

Nonetheless, analyzing law through literary theory and cultural criticism proves troublesome for some lawyers, judges, and even legal scholars.[39] Under this method, legal language "loses its finality and stability of meaning," and the law becomes "open to reinterpretation and critique."[40] Although literary criticism is comfortable with ambiguity and ambivalence, legal analysis is not. For example, Richard A. Posner argues that legal and literary texts should remain distinct, and the difference between the two is rooted in their separate social functions.[41] In *Law and Literature* (1998), Posner explains "we cannot learn a great deal about the day-to-day operations of a legal system from works of imaginative literature."[42] For Posner, law and its body of texts exist as a system of "social control."[43] He argues that while the law's operations may be illuminated by the social sciences and through literary analysis, literature exists as an art form that is best interpreted and evaluated aesthetically.[44]

The difference between literary and legal analysis to which Posner refers rests in the IRAC method that law school students and legal professionals employ. This method analyzes written court opinion by considering the legal issue in question (I), the rule of law (R), the application or analysis of the rule (A), and the conclusion (C). Analyzing the rule depends upon "facts" that identify the legal issue and that explain an experience or observation. Relevant and applicable only to the legal rule in question, human behavior remains confined to these facts for the legal professionals and scholars that use this technique. As Peter Brooks puts it, "thinking like a lawyer involves

37 Kieran Dolin, A Critical Introduction to Law and Literature, loc. 290 (2007) ebook.

38 *Id.* at loc. 291.

39 *Id.* at loc. 297.

40 *Id.* at loc. 297.

41 Richard Posner, Law and Literature: Revised and Enlarged Edition, 5 (1998).

42 *Id.* at 5.

43 *Id.* at 7.

44 *Id.*

divesting yourself of your preconceptions about the rights and wrongs of a case, divesting yourself of your instinctive sense of where justice lies or how fair play should be exercised, in order to learn to analyze human actions in their intersections with law."[45] Therefore, this concept restricts the point of view and negates other social practices, and cultural understandings remain imbedded within the legal narrative of written court opinion.

However, serving a purpose outside the legal profession, analyzing law as literature provides an alternative, multidimensional perspective for legal professionals, scholars, and those seeking an alternative meaning of the law outside of its narrow judicial interpretation. For example, in 1973, James Boyd White organized a field of study—law and literature—that questioned law's narrow interpretation of value. In his textbook *The Legal Imagination* (1973), White suggested that statutes, constitutions, and written court opinion could also be analyzed through critical theory and literary expression, which consider law's larger philosophical or cultural contexts. He argued that legal documents may be read literally—for the purpose of legal discourse, and metaphorically—for the purpose of discerning "social realities."[46] In addition to White, other scholars such as Lenora Ledwon separate law and literature into two parts: law *in* literature and law *as* literature.[47] Law in literature considers legal themes applicable to literary texts that typically tell a legal story, such as Shakespeare's *The Merchant of Venice* (1598) or Harper Lee's *To Kill a Mockingbird* (1962). On the other hand, law as literature applies techniques associated with literary criticism to written court opinion and other legal documents and treatises.

Reading law as literature recognizes the human condition that traditional legal analysis disregards. White encourages reading law as literature, since doing so breaks down the mechanistic barriers of legal analysis and what he defines as "law as machine."[48] In his essay "Imagining the Law" (1996), White distinguishes "law as machine" from "law as rhetoric."[49] "Law as machine" employs the technical IRAC method to analyze law.[50] On the other hand, "law as rhetoric" considers legal language as "an activity of speech … and imagination in a social world."[51] He argues that reading both legal and literary works shares in this notion of imagination: when a person reads a text, he envisions the world the author created. To break the confines of tradi-

45 Peter Brooks, *Law, Literature: Where Are We?* in TEACHING LAW AND LITERATURE, 61, 63 (Austin Sarat et al. eds. 2011).

46 JAMES BOYD WHITE, THE LEGAL IMAGINATION 31 (1973).

47 LENORA LEDWON, LAW AND LITERATURE: TEXT AND THEORY, ix (1996).

48 James Boyd White, *Imagining the Law*, in THE RHETORIC OF LAW 31 (Austin Sarat and Thomas R. Kearns, eds., 1996).

49 *Id.* at 31 and 35.

50 *Id.* at 35.

51 *Id.*

tional legal analysis, White encourages the same kind of imaginative reading with legal writing.[52] Through a close reading, he analyzes classic poems such as John Keats's "Ode to a Grecian Urn" and Emily Dickinson's "A Narrow Fellow." He concludes that imagining the authors' created worlds may invoke "feelings of safety, danger, sympathy with others, feelings that will confirm the reality ... of his own."[53] In this book, I follow White's suggestion of reading law as literature and "imagining" the world in which it was written. Doing so restores a sense of humanity within a legal decision that the IRAC method removes. Reading law as literature provides a rich reflection of not only how we exist within the order of the legal institution but also how we relate to one another in the world we share.

Reading law as literature also examines certain cultural contexts that filter into different texts. In his essay "Human Dignity and the Claim of Meaning: Athenian Tragic Drama and Supreme Court Opinions" (2002), White argues that both the Greek tragedy *Oresteia* and the US Supreme Court opinion *Cohen v. California* (1971) provide a story—a narrative in which the audience must "imagine" the world to discern meaning.[54] Both types of texts bring attention to events, people, and places that otherwise might have been overlooked.[55] For instance, *Oresteia* contextualizes the fall of Troy. In the ancient drama, a hero from the Trojan War returns to Mycenae only to be murdered by his wife and her lover. White argues that the literature brings to light forces or impulses that are normally hidden, educating the Greek audience about its postwar "moral situation."[56] By comparison, *Cohen v. California* (1971) highlights a US Vietnam War protest incident that arose when a demonstrator entered a municipal court building with a shirt that read "F--- the draft." White argues that the law and the drama similarly share in educating the audience by a small piece of the larger picture.[57] Just as the drama examines a murder within the larger context of the Trojan War, the court opinion examines the simple act of protest within the legal context of its political postwar and anti-war debate.[58] Both types of texts then may be viewed as cultural documents "that work to teach the public" through narrative.[59]

52 *Id.* at 31.

53 *Id.*

54 James Boyd White, *Human Dignity and the Claim of Meaning: Athenian Tragic Drama and Supreme Court Opinions*, in 27.1 Journal of Sup Ct Hist 45, 62 (2002).

55 *Id.* at 49.

56 *Id.* at 48.

57 *Id.* at 51.

58 *Id.*

59 *Id.* at 61.

Law, Literature, and Gender Discrimination

Analyzing both law and literature as cultural documents may reveal deep-rooted social attitudes, preconceptions, and biases. By doing so, we also may expose the voices of those who have been historically and culturally silenced—the "individuals and groups structurally excluded from privileged categories."[60] In her essay "Literature, Culture, and Law at Duke University" (2011), Robin West explains that over the past decade, both legal and literary scholars alike have begun to explore ways in which cultural studies may work to "inform our understanding of law" by deconstructing legal reasoning, conveying or challenging its norms, and possibly perverting its meaning by examining the social contexts that influence legal decisions.[61] Like White, West relates law to literature in that both types of writings "interpret community:" both texts may reflect social attitudes about race, gender, and socioeconomic status.[62] Since law and culture interact with one another, "sometimes culture is law" and vice versa.[63] As a result, West argues that law may be negatively influenced by biased social attitudes that could lead to erroneous legal decisions.[64]

To demonstrate how literature, law, and culture intermingle, West argues that both literature and law may demonstrate a commonly held assumption of white male privilege and gender or racial victimization.[65] West compares Tom Wolfe's best-selling novel *I Am Charlotte Simmons* (2004) to a 2006 alleged rape incident that occurred at Duke University. In *I Am Charlotte Simmons*, a poor black woman on an academic scholarship attends a fictional university known for its economic privilege and internationally ranked basketball team. Attempting to fit in with predominantly white students, Charlotte attends a party and is pressured into unwanted and painful sexual intercourse with a male athlete. Victim to the elite society that disregards her humanity and glorifies male athleticism, she loses her integrity, her academic career, and her self-possession in the end.[66] In this sense, *I Am Charlotte Simmons* exposes a longstanding cultural view of the advantages white men possess over women of other races.

In law, such cultural views remain so strong that their implications may negatively and incorrectly affect a legal outcome, creating unjust damage to

60 Elizabeth S. Anker and Bernadette Meyler, *Introduction*, in NEW DIRECTIONS IN LAW AND LITERATURE, 7 (Elizabeth S. Anker and Bernadette Meyler, eds., 2017).

61 Robin West, *Literature, Culture, and Law at Duke University*, in TEACHING LAW AND LITERATURE 98, 104 and 105 (Austin Sarat et al. eds., 2011)

62 *Id.* at 103 and 108.

63 *Id.* at 108.

64 *Id.* at 108.

65 *Id.* at 110.

66 *Id.* at 110.

both victims and perpetrators. West demonstrates this phenomenon by challenging the deep-rooted social perspective of racial oppression and gendered harm with the 2006 Duke case in which a black female exotic dancer falsely accused three white male lacrosse players of raping her.[67] In this case, the university, student body, public, and law enforcement falsely presumed the men's guilt upon the basis of the longstanding belief of systemic racism and misogyny. For example, when the woman initially filed the report, the prosecutor aggressively pursued the case against the men, relying primarily on the woman's report to law enforcement.[68] Other women also began making claims of being raped by Duke athletes, and the media began questioning the men's credibility through print, television, and social media sources.[69] Prior to trial, however, charges were dropped when DNA evidence revealed that none of the members of the lacrosse team could have raped her.[70] In this case, West argues that the law falsely relied on shared cultural impressions of white male superiority and black female inferiority that *I Am Charlotte Simmons* provides: law "was sometimes in competition with ... and sometimes in cooperation with" these deep-rooted beliefs that are reinforced in law, literature, and society.[71]

These well-established cultural beliefs and biased attitudes might be reflected in the "stock stories" in both literature and law. "Stock stories" consist of a basic plotline and standard characters that authors have modified over the centuries to create something new. For example, in a stock story named "The Quest," a hero goes on a long journey and overcomes many obstacles to win a prize or an honor.[72] An example of "The Quest" is found in *The Odyssey*. In another stock story, "The Falsely Accused," the hero must struggle to prove his innocence when he is falsely accused of a crime.[73] An example of this type of stock story would be found in the movie *The Fugitive*.[74] These stock stories and others have become implanted within our culture due to their familiarity and repetition, and they bolster distinct attitudes established within society. *The Odyssey* and *The Fugitive* teach us that a man proves his masculine strength by overcoming unjust treatment and difficult obstacles. The stock story of a black woman wronged by a white society in *I Am Charlotte*

67 *Id.* at 111.

68 *Id.* at 109.

69 *Id.*

70 *Id.*

71 *Id.* at 107.

72 Mike Skotnicki, *Several Types of "Stock Stories" Can Be Used in Persuasive Brief Writing*, BRIEFLY WRITING (May 29, 2012), https://brieflywriting.com/2012/05/29/several-types-of-stock-stories-can-be-used-in-persuasive-briefwriting/

73 *Id.*

74 *Id.*

Simmons (2004) and the 2006 Duke case demonstrate a long tradition of sexism and racism in which both the literary text and the legal case stand.

Gender Bias in Law and Literature

Gender bias implanted within stock stories of both literature and law may uncover social attitudes or assumptions that marginalize and victimize women and other members of minority groups. The stock stories and the cultural attitudes they expose can influence the outcome of a judicial decision if they are applied in law.[75] For example, a stock story about a woman who endures being beaten by her husband over time conveys an attitude of indifference toward domestic violence. In *A Critical Introduction to Law and Literature* (2007), Kieran Dolin examines this type of stock story that reinforces a patriarchal norm that subjugates women to male authority. He argues that the judge in the English Court of Criminal Appeals case, *R v. Duffy* (1949), constructs the law from a masculine perspective and a norm driven by "a set of male social practices."[76] In this historical case, a minimal narrative of the circumstances reveals that the woman had been "subjected to violence" by her husband throughout their marriage.[77] She had wanted to leave but had been forced to stay.[78] When her husband went to sleep one night, she killed him with a hatchet and a hammer.[79] Although the woman had been clearly provoked over the course of time, the judge, Devlin J., did not address provocation but instead relied upon moral discourse within the legal decision:

> A long course of cruel conduct may be more blameworthy than a sudden act of retaliation, but you are not concerned with blame here—the blame attaching to the dead man. You are not standing in judgment on him. He has not been heard in this court. He cannot now ever be heard … It does not matter how cruel he was, … except in so far as it resulted in the final act of the appellant. What matters is whether this girl had time to say: "Whatever I have suffered, whatever I have endured, I know that Thou shalt not kill."[80]

The judge reinforced the stock story of a wife who weathers the storm of ongoing violence from her husband. The cultural attitude implied in the stock story suggests that the wife chooses to tolerate the abuse, and she should live

75 *Id.*
76 R v. Duffy, 1 A11 ER 932 (1949).
77 *Id.*
78 *Id.*
79 *Id.*
80 *Id.*

with whatever consequences arise from her choice. In other words, although the judge suggests otherwise, the woman is in fact blamed for staying in a violent relationship. Although sympathetic to the woman's sufferings, the judge relies upon the stock story to penalize her for her immorality and the "sudden temporary loss of control that is expressed in violence."[81] Here, Dolin argues that the judge neglects a feminine perspective and bases his decision upon a masculine cultural view that reinforces "a hidden bias, an unacknowledged structural fault that excluded battered women from a defense that could have allowed the circumstances leading up to their actions to be taken into account."[82] In this case, the judge's rationale reinforces both the stock story and gender bias toward women.

In this book, I expand Dolin's argument about hidden bias in stock stories that reinforce gender stereotypes and violence against women. I examine acquaintance crimes such as rape, sexual harassment, stalking, and domestic abuse, and I reason that the female victim's physical or psychological "freeze response" is commonly and inaccurately mistaken for her consent. I argue that by ignoring the brain's natural response to trauma, American law that has been historically influenced by a culture of disbelief unjustly blames the victim for her abuse. While literature and legal scholars alike have examined discrimination against women in both fields of study, there is a gap in knowledge: current scholarship does not thematically pair American literature to law, and it does not correlate victim trauma to victim blame. However, by doing so, the synergistic effect between both law and literature provides a powerful statement: a victim does not "ask for it," and she should not arouse suspicions just because she does not fight, run away, or report the incident. Instead, the more common and most practical response demonstrates that she becomes physically and mentally paralyzed by fear and trauma. As a result, she dissociates, shuts down, and most often remains stuck in the fright and captivity of the abuse.

Chapter Summaries

Twenty-first-century American novels have been chosen because few, if any, have been written about these topics until this time. The novels *Thirteen Reasons Why* (2017) and *You* (2018) have recently been made into Netflix series. The rationale for using these novels and the other two is to maintain the stamina of their ongoing messages within popular culture and to insert that content into a space within the academic conversation. Chapter 2: Acquaintance Rape: A Victim's "Freeze Response" Mistaken for Consent

81 Dolin at loc. 491.
82 *Id.*

in *Thirteen Reasons Why* (2007) examines the systemic defect in current American rape law. It demonstrates how the victims in Jay Asher's novel physically "freeze" from fear while being sexually assaulted. It explains that this reaction contradicts current law that encourages a victim to "fight or flee" to prove that she did not consent. The chapter argues that fighting or fleeing is impossible, unwise, or dangerous, and both law and a society that is based on a culture of disbelief unfairly dismiss a victim's typical "freeze" response. Moreover, a victim's "freeze" response is most often mistaken for consent. Particularly with acquaintance rapes, a culture of disbelief also falsely relies on rape myths that inculpate the victim. In this sense, the chapter contends that rape myths contribute to perpetrators' ability to shift blame by using the DARVO technique. It concludes by arguing that a culture of disbelief, the acceptance of rape myths, and DARVO help explain why so few rape cases are prosecuted in the United States and why so many guilty perpetrators go unpunished.

Chapter 3: Domestic Violence: A Victim's Emotional Paralysis Mistaken for Acceptance in *Black and Blue* (1998) investigates the harmful consequences of limiting domestic violence crimes to only include physical abuse or threats of physical harm. Focusing on additional complexities that contain verbal manipulation, financial coercion, threats about the children, isolation, and victim blaming, this chapter examines the severity of hopelessness a victim faces in Anna Quindlen's novel *Black and Blue* (1998). It demonstrates that a victim's indecision to leave does not correlate to her mental instability because she "lets the violence happen" or her propensity to lie about the seriousness of the abuse. Instead, many victims suffer from longstanding psychological trauma that causes them to remain physically and mentally "frozen" and trapped in the privacy of their home with the abuser. Although the victim in *Black and Blue* eventually leaves her perpetrator and goes into hiding, the novel provides an example of a legal system that still fails to protect her and many other victims who suffer from this form of violence.

Chapter 4: Stalking: A Victim's Powerlessness Mistaken for Tolerance in *You* (2014) examines the effects of yet another unproductive symbolic law of stalking. In Caroline Kepnes's novel *You* (2014), the victim does not realize her boyfriend had been stalking her until it is too late. In this case, the novel does not provide a narrative of the legal impediments a victim faces when she attempts to report the stalker. However, the story demonstrates the psychology of a stalker and victimology of his target. To that end, this chapter separately analyzes statutes and court cases to trace the difficulty in reporting the crime and to explain why a stalker can easily get away with it. Although the victim might "fight" and report the crime, the system typically fails her so she cannot "flee" or escape from her stalker. Thus, most often she "freezes" in mental and emotional defeat and resolve to a potential lifetime of fear and danger.

Chapter 5: Sexual Harassment: A Victim's Inaction Mistaken for Acquiescence in *The Boys Club* (2020) analyzes another aspect of law that favors the perpetrator. It traces sexual harassment legislation and court cases to demonstrate that the law most often does not protect victims. Instead, it unjustly relies on and relinquishes power to a corporation's ineffective anti-harassment policy. This chapter also studies Erica Katz's *The Boys Club* (2020) to exemplify toxic masculinity in workplace culture. In the novel, these cultural constructs perpetuate different forms of sexual harassment from older, more experienced men who supervise younger women. Their pernicious behavior ranges from inappropriate jokes and comments to "consensual" affairs with an abuse of power, to nonconsensual sexual harassment, and ultimately to attempted rape. With these and other examples from *The Boys Club,* this chapter contends that adult grooming, a victim's freeze response, and the long-term effects of PTSD are factors that are often mistaken for a victim's permission or consent. Through this process, sexual harassers and predators take advantage of social, organizational, and legal systems that fail to protect victims.

2 Acquaintance Rape

A Victim's "Freeze Response" Mistaken for Consent in *Thirteen Reasons Why* (2007)

In his famous TEDx Talk, Dr. Jackson Katz stated, "We talk about how many women were raped last year, not about how many men raped women."[1] He explained that the reason for this error is because most men mistakenly dismiss crimes against women as "women's issues."[2] In this sense, Katz describes sexual assault within the constraints of a gender binary. Nevertheless, victims of sexual assault may also include men and nonbinary individuals. However, for purposes of this book and of this chapter, I follow Dr. Katz's rationale. I focus on crimes against women and sexual assault since a disproportionate number of victims identify as female and their abusers identify as male. From this perspective, Katz argues that only a few "good men" advocate against these offenses that are otherwise considered within the scope of the "female realm."[3] Notwithstanding, men—who perform the action—primarily engage in these violent behaviors against women that "are tied to definitions of manhood."[4] Yet women—who encounter the harm as victims—unnecessarily carry the burden and the blame for a crime they do not commit and for which they are not responsible. As a result, men have the duty to work together with other men and women to change the system and to put a stop to these gender-based crimes.[5] In other words, Dr. Katz contends that "women's issues" belong in the category of "men's issues."

Some might think that Dr. Katz's call to action could be coming to fruition during our current times where celebrities and public figures are finally being punished for a rape that they committed long ago. In fact, the FBI reported a recent increase of reported rape cases—from approximately 33 percent to

1 Jackson Katz, *Violence Against Women—It's a Men's Issue*, TEDx (Nov. 2012), https://www.ted.com/talks/jackson_katz_violence_against_women_it_s_a_men_s_issue?

2 *Id.*

3 *Id.*

4 *Id.*

5 *Id.*

DOI: 10.4324/9781003303572-2

50 percent.[6] Although these statistics indicate that more victims are stepping forward, still only half of all of them report the crime. Of those women, 20 percent worry about retaliation from both the perpetrator and from a society at large that quickly jumps to conclusions and blames them.[7] Thirteen percent feel that law enforcement will not support or help and, sadly, eight percent believe that the sexual assault was not important enough to report.[8] These statistics reflect upon the historical insignificance with which rape victims have been viewed. As Dr. Katz's claim reflects, society has normalized violent forms of masculine aggression and minimized the degree of severity for which victims suffer. In this chapter, I argue that normalized violence against rape victims contributes to the current culture of disbelief that victims face, and it helps explain the inequity of how rape cases are handled by both law enforcement and the criminal justice system.

Problematic Legal Definition

This problem of the law's ineffectiveness begins with rape legislation, which is an example of a symbolic law that may be in effect (de jure) but is one that is rarely enforced (de facto).[9] Under this type of legislation, some members of law enforcement and the criminal justice system deprioritize these crimes to the point of ignoring them or placing little to no emphasis on investigation. So, although a statute is in place, assailants rarely face consequences for breaking the law. Without these consequences, rapists and other criminals are encouraged to commit more crime, which endangers not only victims but also the public at large.[10] Under these circumstances, there is an increased risk of harm toward law-abiding citizens and a greater dispensation for those who engage in criminal and immoral behaviors.[11]

Located in Black's Law Dictionary, the legal definition of rape that is accepted in most jurisdictions in the United States is defined as

> Unlawful sexual intercourse with a female without her consent. The unlawful carnal knowledge of a woman by a man forcibly and against her will. The act of sexual intercourse committed by a man with a woman not

6 Federal Bureau of Investigation, *2017 Crime in the United States*, Table 1. (2017), https://ucr.fbi.gov/crime-in-the-u.s/2017/crime-in-the-u.s.-2017/tables/table-1

7 Department of Justice, *Criminal Victimization*, Table 1. (2016), https://www.bjs.gov/content/pub/pdf/cv16.pdf

8 *Id.*

9 David John Frank et al., *The Global Dimensions of Rape Reform: A Cross-National Study of Policy Outcomes*, in 74 American Sociological Rev., 272, 272 (2009).

10 Priban, Jiri, *On Legal Symbolism on Symbolic Legislation: A Systems Theoretical Perspective*, *in* Symbolic Legislation Theory and Developments in Biolaw, 105, 105 (2016).

11 *Id.*

> his wife and without her consent, committed when the woman's resistance is overcome by force or fear, or under other prohibitive conditions.[12]

By interpreting this definition alongside a state's rape legislation, the victim (or rather, the criminal prosecutor who works on the victim's behalf) must prove that the defendant forced or threatened to force a victim, and the victim did not consent to sexual intercourse. To meet the highest legal standard for burden of proof—proof beyond a reasonable doubt—a female rape victim proves these elements by either presenting testimony from an eyewitness of the crime or by exhibiting physical, visible evidence of her resistance and struggle against the perpetrator. As Livia Gershon puts it "state laws generally define consent so that victims [have] to physically resist their attackers for the assault to be understood as rape."[13] Compared to other consent crimes such as assault, battery, robbery, or trespass, rape cases are unique in that she must prove both the defendant's misconduct and her own nonconsent.[14] For the victim, this works as a double-edged sword compared to the other crimes because what she did prior, during, or after the rape may be called into question. Under these unique circumstances, both the defendant's and the victim's conduct are "put on trial." When this occurs, the odds rarely work in the victim's favor.

The Origins of the Everyman Rapist in Renaissance England

Up until Queen Elizabeth I's reign in Renaissance England, rape was considered a crime of property and not a crime of person. However, in 1597, rape law changed. What was once a crime of property against a woman's nearest male relative became a crime of person, and "a woman's body in the sexual sense was seen legally to be her own."[15] However, only the most heinous "monster" rape cases were brought to trial, and most victims continued to suffer in silence.[16] Therefore, the concept of believing an accused rapist over his victim begins with longstanding culturally accepted archetypes that polarize monster rapists from everyman rapists. According to Garthine Walker, monster rapists were defined as those who rape and enforce an excessive amount of violence, engage in gang rape, or commit an additional crime.[17] These types

12 Henry Campbell Black, Black's Law Dictionary With Pronunciations. 10 ed. (2014).

13 Livia Gershon, *How Reforms to Rape Law Changed Our Understanding of the Crime*, JSTOR Daily (Sept. 25, 2016), https://daily.jstor.org/rape-law-reforms-made-rape-visible/

14 Susan Estrich, *Rape*, in Feminist Jurisprudence 177, (Patricia Smith, ed. 1993).

15 Marion Wynne-Davies, *The Swallowing Womb: Consumed and Consuming Women in Titus Andronicus*, in The Matter of Difference: Materialist Feminist Criticism of Shakespeare 129, 131 (Valerie Wayne,,ed., 1991).

16 Lee A. Ritscher, The Seminotics of Rape in Renaissance English Literature, 9 (2009).

17 Depending upon the nature and severity of the rape, English Renaissance law and society polarized rapists into either the "monster" or the "everyman." Garthine Walker, *Everyman or a Monster? The Rapist in Early Modern England, c.1600–1750, in* 76.1 History Workshop Journal, 5, 18 (2013).

of criminals were unequivocally punished due to their exceeding the "normal" bounds of sexual activity and to their leaving a distinguishing injury on the woman's body (e.g., bruises, cuts, swellings, etc.).[18] The monster rapists then overextended acceptable notions of masculine vigor by committing an additional offense and/or by visibly wounding the victim.

By contrast, the everyman rapist was not viewed as a hardened criminal or degenerate in society. He was an everyday, hardworking, typically law-abiding citizen who most often got away with raping a woman. Instead of leaving physical proof of the rape, he surreptitiously forced himself onto a woman. Often, he and the victim were acquainted. Under these circumstances, the everyman rapist typically escaped legal punishment since his behavior was frequently dismissed as normal masculine aggression or an acceptable means of seducing the female. Because of these allowances, the everyman rapist could strong-arm a woman into having sex with him:

> When rape was viewed as the expression of overwhelming male desire and frustrated passions, it was easily situated on a spectrum on which it shaded into normal sexual behavior ... A degree of sexual aggression, after all, constituted "healthy masculinity and male sexuality." Many men who coerced women through violence or threats or pestering were considered to be "just men" doing what men did naturally; women should simply deal with and deflect such behaviour as best they could.[19]

In English Renaissance courts, the crime of rape became problematic when "the lines between rape, coercion, persuasion and seduction were variously drawn, and individuals disagreed on where particular incidents fell."[20] So everyman rapists could not only easily acquit themselves when the rape proved ambiguous, but also these men could refute rape charges by expressing an irresistible impulse.[21] For instance, in three court cases from 1570 to 1650, the excuse of "overbearing desire" proved successful when the accused used the "irresistible male lust and love" justification.[22] This defense coincided with the idea that men could not control their desire, but instead, females were to blame: victims were frequently stereotyped as either aggressive "harpies" who "asked for it" or simple-minded creatures who were "lured" into being raped by men who possessed excessive sexual appetites.[23]

18 *Id.* at 20.
19 *Id.* at 13.
20 *Id.* at 11.
21 *Id.* at 13.
22 *Id.*
23 *Id.* at 4.

USEEOC v. Hometown Buffet (2008) and the Monster Rapist

Current-day America and Renaissance England not only share the idea that women may be responsible for the everyman rape. US courts tend to also punish only the monster rapists who visibly injure the victim or who also commit an additional crime. For example, in *USEEOC v. Hometown Buffet* (2008), although Mr. Carzola and Ms. Lopez knew one another from work, he stole her house keys and entered her home without permission.[24] Covering his face and attempting to disguise his voice, he threatened to kill Ms. Lopez with a knife.[25] He then dragged her into the living room, tied her hands, threatened to murder her young son, and then raped her.[26] In this case, the California court stated that the "background facts regarding the rape are largely undisputed" and the testimony indicated both nonconsent and threat of force.[27] Entering her apartment without permission, he distinctly premeditated the crime since he also took her keys, threatened her life with a deadly weapon, and tied her hands. By these actions, the court determined that Mrs. Lopez could not physically resist while he held her at knife point with her hands tied. The court inferred nonconsent since Mr. Carzola physically threatened not only Ms. Lopez, but also her child, who witnessed the crime. In this instance, Mr. Carzola completely overcame Ms. Lopez, and he committed additional crimes such as theft, breaking and entering of her home, and assault with a deadly weapon. So, when other misdemeanors or felonies occur during this type of monster rape, these crimes lend to the probative value of a rape conviction.[28] As a result, like English Renaissance law, US courts most readily convict these monster rapists.[29]

24 United States Equal Employment Opportunity Commission (EEOC) v. Hometown Buffet, U.S. Dist., 3:06-cv02150-JM-JMA, S.D. Cal., (2008).

25 *Id.*

26 *Id.*

27 *Id.*

28 In Texas and other states, "the emphasis is still put on physical force, violence, and coercion. But these scenarios do not always reflect reality: only about 10% to 12% of victims report they were physically injured or threatened during sexual assault." Hamdan, Nadia, *The Probability Gap: Why It's Hard for Prosecutors to Prove Rape Cases Beyond a Reasonable Doubt*, Crime and Justice: Austin's NPR Station (Aug. 2019) https://www.kut.org/crime-justice/2019-08-20/the-provability-gap-why-its-hard-for-prosecutors-to-prove-rape-cases-beyond-a-reasonable-doubt. A recent study conducted by criminology professors Melissa S. Morabito, Linda M. Williams, and April Pattavina indicated that fewer than 7 percent of reported rape cases in the United States result in a conviction (III). One main reason is because there are no physical signs of injury, no weapon was involved, no witnesses were present, and the evidence relies on his word against hers (VI). Morabito, Melissa S., Linda M. Williams, and April Pattavina, *Decision Making in Sexual Assault Cases: Replication Research on Sexual Violence Case Attrition in the US*, US Department of Justice Office of Justice Programs' National Criminal Justice Reference Service, 1, 1, 2019.

29 See *USEEOC v. Hometown Buffet* (2008), where Mr. Carzola received a 42-year sentence.

Problems with Acquaintance Rapes

Yet the scenario in *USEEOC v. Hometown Buffet* is an atypical one, as most everyman rapists do not commit an additional felony and thus engage in "acquaintance rapes."[30] When the defendant and victim know one another, the element of consent may become unclear because although there might be physical evidence from a rape kit, it's one testimony against the other.[31] In these cases, conflicting stories exist without the presence of physical signs of her struggle like broken bones, lacerations, or bruises.[32] Without these signs of resistance, the criminal justice system's standard of proof is not met. As a result, rape convictions are quite rare compared to other crimes: a 2017 survey from RAINN (Rape, Abuse, and Incest National Network) revealed that for every 230 rapes that are reported to law enforcement, only 5 result in a criminal conviction.[33]

Rape Culture and Rape Myths

Historically, female rape victims have not been supported by the criminal justice system due to shared ideas from a dominant part of a patriarchal society that has normalized violent crimes against women. Anchoring itself on longstanding stereotypes, a rape culture originates from those notions such as "men should lead and women should follow" and "women may be used for pleasure and disposal."[34] Reinforced in the media, movies, music, and popular culture, the patriarchy views women as objects, not individual people with thoughts and feelings. Subject to the masculine gaze, girls become conditioned to believe that if a boy likes her, he is mean to her. As adolescents and teenagers, females become very familiar with the stigmatizing good girl/bad girl juxtaposition. Pejorative labels like "tease," "slut," "whore," and "bitch," heavily impact how the girls are viewed amongst school peers. In turn, the idea that women are generally inferior to men conditions girls and later women for abuse in schools, in their homes, in their workplaces, and in their romantic

30 The Department of Justice: Office of Justice Program, which states that 70 percent of all rapes are acquaintance rapes and 90 percent of those victims do not report the crime; *Department of Justice, Criminal Victimization*, Revised. Table 1 (2016), https://www.bjs.gov/content/pub/pdf/cv16.pdf

31 See *People v. Evans* (1979) and *Goldberg v. State* (1979). In both cases, the courts indicated that for a victim to prove that she did not consent to having sex with the defendant, she must show "physical, severe signs of struggle." These signs of struggle include significant injuries such as bruises, broken bones, or lacerations.

32 *Id.*

33 RAINN, *Victims of Sexual Violence Statistics*, (2017), https://www.rainn.org/statistics/victims-sexual-violence

34 Marshall University, *Rape Culture*, Women's and Gender Center: Marshall University, (2021), https://www.marshall.edu/wcenter/sexual-assault/rape-culture/

relationships. From this line of reasoning, patriarchy easily transverses into sexism, and a rape culture thrives "through the use of misogynistic language, the objectification of women's bodies, and the glamorization of sexual violence, thereby creating a society that disregards women's rights and safety."[35] As Fredrikson and Roberts put it, "everyday commonplace forms of sexual objectification" quickly turns into forms of sexual victimization that underscore a forced double-standard that is placed on women, but not men.[36]

Consequently, certain myths may further contribute to the blame-shifting, knee-jerk reaction that automatically places the victim's credibility into question. Deriving from the good girl/bad girl stereotype that emphasizes her sexuality, this form of objectification crosses a very thin line into excusing sexual violence and abuse. In a court of law, rape myths may be used to muddy the waters of consent, and the prosecutor may not be able to prove each element "beyond a reasonable doubt." Yet whether used in a court of law or observed in our everyday lives, common rape myths contribute to the idea that women "ask for it," and deserve to be raped.[37] For example, the "token resistance" rape myth encourages rough, aggressive, or violent forms of seduction—a woman means "yes" when she says "no" to sexual advances.[38] Similar to "no means yes," "she asked to be raped" makes excuses such as "she was walking at night by herself," "she is promiscuous or flirtatious," "she was drinking alcohol," or "she was looking to be raped in that outfit."[39] Even other rape myths extol the rapist's good looks or reputably good behavior and use those characteristics to automatically exonerate him: "an attractive guy like that does not need to rape anyone" or "oh he would never do that."[40] Even more so, another rape myth rationalizes that date rape is just "sex that a woman regrets in the morning."[41] Under the reasoning of all these rape myths, the victim is portrayed as either negligent or beguiling, and she explicitly or implicitly lures the perpetrator into raping her. Ultimately, she unjustly maintains culpability for his violent sexual actions against her.

35 *Id.*

36 Barbara L. Fredrickson and Tomi Ann Roberts, *Objectification Theory: Toward Understanding Women's Lived Experiences and Mental Health Risks*, 21 Psy Women Quart., 179, 179 (1997).

37 Katie M. Edwards, et al., *Rape Myths: History, Individual and Institutional-Level Presence, and Implications for Change*. 65 Sex Roles, 761, 761 (2011).

38 Sabiene Silke, Reading Rape: The Rhetoric of Sexual Violence in American Literature and Culture, 1790–1990, 9–10 (2002). According to Silke, verbally and physically aggressive forms of masculine seduction that encourage women to "give in" to sexual advances are intertwined amongst and within American rape myths and rape culture.

39 Diane C. Carmody and Lekeshia M. Washington, *Rape myth acceptance among college women: The impact of race and prior victimization*, 16 Journal of Interpersonal Violence 452, 452 (2001).

40 Katie Harding, Asking for It: The Alarming Rise of Rape Culture—and What We Can Do About It 6 (2015).

41 *Id.*

Another rape myth of which the #MeToo movement has recently raised awareness includes the "lying woman," which reasons that women are out to destroy men so they make up lies about being raped. In this sense, the woman involved is cast as a " suspect subject' ... who historically has been socially constituted not only as someone who lies, but indeed as someone who is a liar at her core."[42] By relying upon this sexist, harmful myth, the patriarchy grossly overestimates the number of false reports when according to a survey by the National Sexual Violence Resource Center, only a miniscule 2 percent exist.[43] Yet through the media, famous men, political figures, actors, or athletes further facilitate the popularity of being falsely accused. As attorney and scholar Susan Estrich puts it, "the myth of the lying woman is the most powerful myth in the tradition of rape law."[44] Due to its notoriety and repeated exposure, this myth dangerously contributes to the general public's fallacious belief that most reported rapes are false and that the victims should not be trusted. Moreover, many men who validate the "lying woman" response assert that they should be frightened and protect themselves against these women who are out to ruin them.[45] Creating widespread panic based on untruths, these men claim that if they do not do so, they should fear being "MeToo'd."[46] In other words, they participate in a fraudulent form of reverse

42 Banet-Weiser, Sarah, *'Ruined Lives: 'Mediated White Male Victimhood*, 24.1 European Journal of Cultural Studies, 63, 63 (2019).

43 National Sexual Violence Resource Center, *False Reporting*, (2012), https://www.nsvrc.org/sites/default/files/Publications_NSVRC_Overview_False- Reporting.pdf

44 Cannold, Leslie, *Sexual Assault and the Myth of the Lying Victim*, ABC News, (2011), https://www.abc.net.au/religion/sexual-assault-and-the-myth-of-the-lying-victim/10101332

45 A 2019 study that took place after the #MeToo movement had gained momentum revealed a backlash of reluctance of men to engage with women at work: "19% of men said they were reluctant to hire attractive women, 21% said they were reluctant to hire women for jobs involving close interpersonal interactions with men (jobs involving travel, say), and 27% said they avoided one-on-one meetings with female colleagues." Atwater, Leanne, et al., *Looking Ahead: How What We Know About Sexual Harassment Now Informs Us of the Future,* Harvard Business Review, (Sept.–Oct. 2019).

46 Former President Donald Trump defended Supreme Court nominee Brett Kavanaugh, and stated that the "#MeToo movement was 'very dangerous' and unfairly threatened powerful men" (Rucker et al.). This statement not only cast doubt upon the women who accused Kavanagh but also the countless women who have claimed sexual assault against other prominent men, which includes Trump himself (Rucker et al.). To that end, in May 2023, a New York civil court determined that Trump was liable for sexual abuse and for raping the victim, E. Jean Carroll (Weiser, et al.). The jury instructed Trump to pay Carroll $5 million in damages (Weiser et al.). Although "more than a dozen women have accused Trump of sexual misconduct over the years, Carroll's allegation was the first to be confirmed by a jury" (Weiser et al.). Phillip Rucker et al., *Defending Kavanaugh, Trump Laments #MeToo as 'Very Dangerous' for Powerful Men*, The Washington Post, (Sept. 2018), https://www.washingtonpost.com/politics/defending-kavanaugh-trump-laments-metoo-as-very-dangerous-for-powerful-men/2018/09/26/e9116536-c1a4-11e8-97a5-ab1e46bb3bc7_story.htmlBenjamin Weiser, et al., *Donald Trump Sexually Abused and Defamed E. Jean Carroll, Jury Finds,* The New York Times, (May 9, 2023), https://www.nytimes.com/live/2023/05/09/nyregion/trump-carroll-rape-trial-verdict

victimization that maintains the current rape culture of disbelief and places future victims in danger. Allison Phipps explains this phenomenon as an effort to restore the authority and influence of typically powerful white men who fear their loss of entitlement.[47] Threatened by the #MeToo movement's success in shifting the narrative, these men attempt to "wrestle back the hegemonic gender stability" by taking on "the mantle of victimhood themselves."[48]

Rape Myths and DARVO

The "lying woman" rape myth and others help establish the ease by which a sexual assault perpetuator deflects responsibility and shifts blame to the victim. According to Harsey and Freyd, these offenders often use a manipulation tactic referred to as DARVO (Deny, Attack, Reverse Victim and Offender) to distract from their own misconduct and to inculpate the victim instead.[49] With DARVO, "perpetuators deny … their involvement in wrongdoing, attack their victims' credibility, and argue they are the real victims."[50] In this sense, perpetrators begin blame shifting with defending: they either deny or diminish their wrongdoing by relying on rape myths and by saying such things as "she's lying," "this did not happen," "I did not rape her," or "she consented to having sex with me." Then they accuse the victim by attacking her character, using "insults, threats, gaslighting, or manipulation to discredit the victim's account of the abuse."[51] By reversing the victim and offender, abusers "switch roles, arguing they are the real victim."[52] In this sense, abusers often make statements based on rape myths such as "she is out to get me," "she is trying to destroy me and/or my family," or "she is trying to ruin my reputation." Regardless of the specifics, abusers reverse victim and offender to "deflect … to switch gears and remove attention from [their own] problematic behavior."[53] In the end, especially with acquaintance rapes, these perpetrators oftentimes prove

47 Although famous, wealthy men of color such as Bill Cosby, R. Kelly, and Aziz Ansari have been accused of rape, the majority of high-profile cases involve white men. ALISON PHIPPS, ME NOT YOU: THE TROUBLE WITH MAINSTREAM FEMINISM 1, (2020).

48 Sarah Banet-Weiser, *'Ruined Lives:' Mediated White Male Victimhood,* 24.1 EUROPEAN JOURNAL OF CULTURAL STUDIES, 60, 60 (2019).

49 Sarah J. Harsey and Jennifer J. Freyd, *The Influence of Deny, Attack, Reverse Victim and Offender and Insincere Apologies on Perceptions of Sexual Assault,* JOURNAL OF INTERPERSONAL VIOLENCE 1, 1 (2023).

50 *Id.* at 1.

51 Lakeisha Fleming, *How Narcissists Use DARVO to Avoid Accountability,* VERYWELL MIND (Aug. 2023), https://www.verywellmind.com/protecting-yourself-from-darvo-abusive-behavior-7562730#:~:text=What%20Does%20DARVO%20Look%20Like%3F,-Knowing%20the%20definition%20of%20DARVO

52 *Id.*

53 *Id.*

successful due to a culture of disbelief that accepts rape myths, and they use DARVO to both confuse and ultimately silence their victims.[54]

Rape Myths, Institutional DARVO, and the Law

DARVO may be adopted not only by individual perpetrators, but also by institutions—whether they be legal, corporate, business, educational, religious, or societal. Institutional DARVO begins with institutional betrayal, which refers to "wrongdoings perpetuated by an institution upon individuals [who are] dependent on that institution."[55] It occurs when an institution fails to prevent misconduct, or it neglects to respond to or support the victims that the institution is designed to protect. In the case of sexual assault, when both a perpetrator and an institution rely on rape myths and blame shifting, institutional DARVO arises.[56] One example of how the "the lying woman" rape myth and institutional DARVO filter into legal reasoning is found in a 2014 Dallas, Texas probation hearing, *The State of Texas v. Sir Khalil Young.*[57] In this case, the defendant, Mr. Young, admitted to raping the victim, who was 14 years old at the time.[58] However, when the judge could have sentenced him for up to 20 years in prison, she sentenced him to only 45 days in jail and a 5-year probation.[59] Additionally, if he successfully completed his probation, the conviction would be wiped from his record.[60]

In an interview with the *Dallas Morning News*, the judge explained the rationale for her light punishment, which reinforced institutional DARVO within the criminal justice system. Namely, the judge reasoned the victim's medical records indicated that she had had several sexual partners and had given birth.[61] As a result, the judge formulated a biased moral value judgment. She indicated that the victim was promiscuous and not "who she claimed to

54 Sarah J. Harsey, Eilleen L. Zurbriggen, and Jennifer J. Freyd, *Perpetuator Responses to Victim Confrontation: DARVO and Victim Self Blame,* 26.6 Journal of Aggression, Maltreatment, and Trauma 644, 644 (2017).

55 Jennifer J. Freyd, *Institutional Betrayal and Institutional Courage,* Freyd Dynamics Lab (Aug. 23, 2023), https://dynamic.uoregon.edu/jjf/institutionalbetrayal/#introduce

56 *Id.*

57 Nick Valencia, *Judge Under Fire for Rape Sentence, Implying Victim Was Promiscuous*, CNN.com. (May 5, 2014) https://www.cnn.com/2014/05/05/justice/texas-rape-sentence/index.ht

58 *Id.*

59 *Id.*

60 Emily, Jennifer, *Judge Says 14 Year-Old Sexual Assault Victim 'Wasn't the Victim She Claimed to Be,* 'Dallas News Powered by Dallas Morning News (2014), https://www.dallasnews.com/news/crime/2014/05/01/judge-says-sexually-assaulted-14-year-old-wasn-t-the-victim-she-claimed-to-be

61 Nick Valencia, *Judge Under Fire for Rape Sentence, Implying Victim Was Promiscuous*, CNN.com. (May 5, 2014) https://www.cnn.com/2014/05/05/justice/texas-rape-sentence/index.html

be."[62] In this case, even though Mr. Young himself admitted his guilt, the judge employed the "no means yes" and the "lying woman" rape myths to rationalize her decision. The judge, as representative of the criminal justice system, failed the victim it was designed to protect, and institutional DARVO occurred. Specifically, the judge believed the victim was indiscriminate (Deny). To that end, the victim then somehow contributed to being raped (Attack), and the defendant deserved little, if any penalty for his wrongdoing (Reverse Victim and Offender). According to scholar Jesse Elvin, the concept of judges stereotyping rape victims and reinforcing rape myths is an all-too-common practice.[63] As he puts it, certain judges "employ crude and problematic sexual stereotypes on their judgments."[64] When this happens as in the case of *Sir Khalil Young*, the victim is condemned, not the perpetrator. In short, DARVO—whether initiated by the perpetrator or an institution—"acts as an agent" to reinforce both rape culture and sexual violence.[65]

The Ineffectiveness of Rape Shield Laws

Rape-shield laws were created to protect the victim from such bias of the law; however, the *Sir Khalil Young* case provides an example of how they may be easily circumvented. Although these laws work to exclude evidence from a victim's past sexual history, "such evidence ... is routinely worked into case proceedings."[66] For example, *Commonwealth v. Berkowitz* (1994) explains that each state enacts a version of a rape shield law that forbids inadmissible behavior, reputation, and opinion as evidence regarding a victim's past sexual conduct.[67] Notwithstanding, the exception to the rule allows evidence of past sexual conduct to prove consent.[68] So the overall goal of the rape-shield laws is to prevent a sexual-assault trial from devolving to an attack on the victim's sexual history. Yet this protective measure most often backfires when the defendant demonstrates the necessity of presenting evidence for purposes of proving consent. Thus, the victim's behavior prior to the rape or her "reputation" might be called into question by "often requir[ing her] literally to air [her] dirty linen in public."[69] The defense uses this past character evidence to place the victim "on trial" by asserting that her presumed promiscuity suggests she had consensual sex with him, and he did not rape

62 *Id.*
63 Jesse Elvin, *The Continuing Use of Problematic Sexual Stereotypes in Judicial Decision-Making*, 18 Feminist Legal Studies 275, 275 (2010).
64 *Id.*
65 Harsey and Freyd at 15.
66 Susan Caringella, Addressing Rape Reform in Law and Practice 32 (2009).
67 Commonwealth v. Berkowitz. 641 A.2d 1161 Pa. (1994).
68 *Id.*
69 Joanna Bourke, Rape : Sex, Violence, History 16 (2007).

her.[70] This information can then be used to instill reasonable doubt, minimize wrongdoing, and exonerate an otherwise guilty defendant. Due to this legal loophole, protection under rape-shield laws typically becomes null and void; broad discretionary interpretation and loosely enforced evidentiary standards often allow for "secondary victimization."[71]

Rape Myths and Victim Blame in *Thirteen Reasons Why* (2007)

The notion of victim blame through rape myths is exemplified in the 2007 young adult novel *Thirteen Reasons Why*.[72] The novel begins with the protagonist, Hannah Baker, having committed suicide. However, prior to her death, an anonymous friend promised to posthumously circulate some cassette tapes to a select group of classmates. The audience learns that Hannah used the tapes to narrate different stories about students who she feels had contributed to the deep depression that led to her killing herself. The horrifying stories offer dark glimpses into the life of what was once a lovely, vibrant, intelligent young woman. We learn that initially, Hannah was new to the town of Crestmont. She moved there with her parents, who were the new owners of the town's pharmacy. Yet over the course of a year at Liberty High, she was ruthlessly teased, bullied, sexually harassed, raped, and tormented into a world of complete darkness. Through Hannah's stories, we see the unforgiving, cruel side of high school, where female "reputations" are constantly being built up or torn down and are at the existence of identity and self-worth. In this case, stories are blown out of proportion, and vicious rumors about Hannah being a "slut" freely circulate.[73] Any friend she attempts to make seems to betray her. As her dignity and mental health continue to deplete, one night she witnesses the rape of classmate Jessica Davis by a fellow male student, Bryce Walker, who had sexually harassed and bullied Hannah and other girls in the past. Out of fear, Hannah does not intervene, and it further contributes

70 According to Reeves Sanday, "Rape is one of the few charges in the criminal justice system where reasonable doubt is induced not so much by the character of the evidence as by fantasies regarding the [victim's] motives for bringing the charges" (xiii). Commonly, juries tend to ignore a prosecutor's evidence of force and/or nonconsent and instead favor the defense's suggestion that the victim agreed to "rough sex" as her past sexual behaviors suggest promiscuity (xiii). Peggy Reeves Sanday, A Woman Scorned: Acquaintance Rape on Trial xiii (1997).

71 Bourke at 16.

72 *Thirteen Reasons Why* was adapted into a popular Netflix series in 2017. The first season of the series closely follows the novel. However, the second season in 2018 and the third season 2019 has evolved from the original story. Why I mention this is because it might become easy to confuse the series with the novel. Nonetheless, I wish to emphasize that I am strictly focusing on the literary analysis of the novel.

73 Jay Asher, Thirteen Reasons Why 23 (2007).

to her heavy guilt, self-deprecation, and deep depression. Ironically in the end, she is also raped by Bryce, the cruel bully, misogynist, sexual harasser, and assaulter. Shortly thereafter, she kills herself. In a sense, Bryce Walker and his kind win.

Sexual Harassment and Rape Myths in *Thirteen Reasons Why*

The novel not only gives a clear picture of the brutality of date rape, but it also provides an example of the severity of the double standard. Specifically, a female's reputation amongst her peers as being "promiscuous" justifies her being sexually harassed. In Hannah's case, her status as the "new girl" started with a vicious rumor about her being "felt up" by her crush, Justin Foley.[74] In fact the only thing that had occurred was that Hannah received her first kiss while on their date at the playground. Nothing else happened, and the two never dated again. However, "she was so new to school that the rumors overshadowed" anything else that anyone knew about her.[75] From that point, gossip amongst her classmates began to justify Hannah's sullied reputation that was ultimately based on a lie.

After Justin's rumor, a "Who's Hot and Who's Not" list circulated, with Hannah being named as "Best Ass in the Freshman Class."[76] While perhaps crudely complimentary at first, this label only caused her classmates to further objectify and depersonalize her. Through the list, the "she asked for it" myth began to originate as she became reduced to a sex object. For example, believing the "Best Ass in the Freshman Class" nomination gave him permission to inappropriately touch her, one classmate named Wally roughly grabbed her wrist and "smacked her ass" in front of some of her classmates at the convenience store one day.[77] Although she attempted to defend herself by knocking Wally's hand away, Hannah had already begun to become a victim of "token resistance." Through the development of Hannah becoming known as "sexually easy," Wally felt entitled to treat her in any manner he saw fit. As Hannah herself admitted, both Justin's rumor and the "Best Ass in the Freshman Class" incident gave "some people the go-ahead to treat [her] like she [was] nothing but that specific body part."[78] Thus, she became victim to rough and aggressive forms of seduction, and when she clearly said "no," Wally and some of her other classmates took it as a "yes."

74 *Id.* at 29.
75 *Id.* at 30.
76 *Id.* at 29.
77 *Id.* at 45.
78 *Id.* at 48.

As the rumors built upon one another, the severity of harassment amongst her male peers and the disregard of viewing Hannah as anything besides a "slut" increased. In another incident that followed, a popular classmate, Marcus Cooley, convinced Hannah to go on a date with him, but she later found out that his intention was just to sexually harass her at a local diner. Specifically, shortly after he met her on the date, he pinned her up against a booth and aggressively grabbed her inner thigh, refusing to let go. Frightened, Hannah fought to "pry [his] fingers away and she told him to stop."[79] When he did not do so, she pushed him out of the booth. Leaving her scared and flustered at his unwanted advances, Marcus loudly called her a "tease" so other classmates who overheard could start yet another vicious cycle of rumors.[80] As a result, she continued to lose any sense of agency she possessed amongst many of her peers. Although Hannah was the victim of intimidation, threats, and sexual harassment, she became condemned and blamed for the wrongdoers' inappropriate, harmful, and aggressive behavior toward her.

Along with Marcus and Wally, Bryce Walker also believed that many girls at school were his to mistreat and abuse in any way he saw fit. Bryce, the most popular athlete and class leader, was known for always getting what he wanted with bad behavior—including being "rough" with girls.[81] Although he was attractive, one female classmate darkly and surreptitiously told Hannah that he was only cute "on the outside."[82] Yet due to his popularity and clout, many classmates feared him since he was well known for bullying, intimidation, and sexual harassment. Everyone knew who he was, and "everyone [knew] what he [did]."[83] Yet no one attempted to undermine him. Both male and female classmates either unwillingly accepted his bad behavior due to fear or went along with it due to peer pressure.

Both the normalization and the extent of Bryce's power and intimidation over his classmates became exemplified when Bryce's friend, Justin Foley, allowed Bryce to rape an unconscious classmate, Jessica Davis. At a party one evening where students were drinking alcohol, Jessica became drunk to the point of incoherence. Justin led Jessica upstairs to what they thought was an empty bedroom, but Hannah was sitting alone on the floor, out of sight and in the dark. When Justin realized that Jessica was almost unconscious and "was not in a romantic mood," he left.[84] However, before Hannah could get up to leave, Hannah heard Bryce outside the door, coaxing Justin into "having a few minutes" with Jessica.[85] Scared of Bryce, Hannah then took the

79 *Id.* at 142.
80 *Id.* at 144.
81 *Id.* at 129.
82 *Id.*
83 *Id.* at 263.
84 *Id.* at 223.
85 *Id.* at 225.

opportunity to quickly hide in the closet. Although Justin initially protested, he ultimately gave in and allowed Bryce to enter the dark room, and he closed the door behind him. Hannah then witnessed Bryce rape an unconscious Jessica through the slats of the closet door.

Rape Culture and Toxic Masculinity

According to Keith Thomas, one of the reasons why some adolescent boys might feel enabled to sexually harass and assault girls without consent is because "key messages about manhood that boys absorb from the culture" not only include that women should be viewed as sexual objects but also "that [boys] meet conflict with aggression, harden themselves, [and] suppress all human emotion except anger."[86] Deriving from patriarchy and sexism, these negative facets of overinflated masculine traits contribute to a form of "toxic masculinity" that discourages young men to process and express their emotions in a healthy manner.[87] Instead, boys are pressured to act "tough" or "hard," and they are rewarded and admired for it. Yet consequently, according to Jackson Katz, the assimilation of the "tough-guy" persona results in men who commit 90 percent of all violent crimes.[88] This form of toxic masculinity also contributes to a rape culture where 95 percent of all imprisoned rapists are also men.[89]

The hyperaggressive "alpha" males like Bryce, who are handsome, athletic, intimidating, and wealthy, are often admired by the public and viewed as the ideal "powerful" man. These men have leadership qualities that allow them to influence others through respect or fear. They also set the standard for toxically masculine behaviors and are capable of either revering or ostracizing members of their peer group. So, when a young man such as Justin does not stand up to his friend who makes harmful sexual advances toward a classmate, he does so because he fears the consequences of appearing "soft."[90] As Dr. Katz explains, most male bystanders do not help a victim who is being harassed or sexually assaulted due to social fear, not physical fear.[91] In this case, spectators dread the aftermath of appearing "weak" if they question or reject toxically masculine behaviors and those who embody them. So, like Justin, these males either refuse to defy the leader or, like Wally and Marcus, they

86 Keith Thomas, The Empathy Gap (Media Education Foundation Video 2015).

87 Jackson Katz et al. Tough Guise (Media Education Foundation Video 1999). Andrea Waling, *Problematizing 'Toxic' and 'Healthy' Masculinity for Addressing Gender Inequalities*, 34.101 Australian Feminist Studies, 362, 362 (2019).

88 Katz, et al. Tough Guise.

89 *Id.*

90 Jackson Katz, The Bystander Moment (Media Education Foundation Video 2018).

91 *Id.*

reinforce the misogynist conduct to try to stand out, impress others, and be more like the alpha-male leader.

Acquaintance Rape and the Unconscious Victim

In *Thirteen Reasons Why,* the rape of Jessica Davis is considered a "date rape" or an "acquaintance rape" since Bryce and Jessica know each other from school.[92] Typically under the circumstances of date rape, the legal element of consent might be difficult to prove since there most likely will not be visible evidence of her struggle against the perpetrator. However, in this case, the fact that Jessica was unconscious from consuming too much alcohol proves that she had the inability to consent to having sex with Bryce. As criminal attorney Michael S. Berg puts it, "it is illegal to engage in sexual intercourse with an individual who is unable to give their consent, such as when they are unconscious from alcohol or drugs."[93] So, under these circumstances, since Jessica was unable to consent to having sex, he raped her. Yet in a sense, the rape myth "she asked for it" confounds this notion and instead reinforces the idea that since she was intoxicated, she somehow contributed to his taking advantage of her. Although contradictory to the legal element of consent, the socially constructed rape myth reinforces both Bryce's mindset and how society oftentimes views victims; she deserved to be raped because she drank too much, and Bryce had every right to do so.

Acquaintance Rape, Consent, and the Law

Although an unconscious Jessica's nonconsent is undeniable, the legal element of consent has a longstanding history of being the most difficult to prove "beyond a reasonable doubt." For example, *People v. Evans* (1975) begins with a scenario in which the defendant met the victim for the first time and offered her a ride home from the airport. The defendant pretended he was a therapist conducting research on women's and men's interactions in singles bars. He took the victim to a singles bar then later to one of his alleged offices. After some time, he advanced upon her, and she rejected him. However, he responded, "Look where you are. You are in the apartment of a strange man. How do you know that I am really who I say I am? How do you know that

92 Miranda Horvath and Jennifer Brown, Rape: Challenging Contemporary Thinking 17 (2009). According to Horvath and Brown, "date rape" may be defined as a rape between two "non-romantic" friends, acquaintances, or colleagues or a rape between two people who have shared a romantic or sexual relationship. In this case, the first type of date rape—a rape between two acquaintances—occurs between Bryce and Jessica.

93 Michael S. Berg, *Rape of an Unconscious Person,* Criminal Law (2018): https://criminallaw.com/categories/crimes-against-a-person/rape-of-an-unconscious-person

I am really a psychologist?" Then, he went on and said, "I could kill you. I could rape you. I could hurt you physically."[94] However, he then quickly changed his narrative and told her that she reminded him of a lost love, which intermittently engaged her sympathies, but then he grabbed her and allegedly raped her.

Based on this testimony, the New York Supreme court determined that, since the victim "offered very little resistance" and "there was no torn clothing, there were no scratches, [and] there were no bruises," the victim consented to have sex with the defendant.[95] In this case, his coercive threats were not enough to imply that he forced her to have sex with him. The court also went on to describe the victim as an "unworldly girl ... incredibly gullible, trusting, and naïve."[96] Although the court made no mention of the victim's actual age, bringing up these characteristics—which had nothing to do with the defendant's misconduct—implied that the credulous victim placed herself in a questionable position with an experienced marauder. Thus, the court evinced the victim's guilt due to her inexperience and lack of knowledge. In other words, the court employed a form of the "she asked for it" rape myth.

In addition to shifting blame to the victim, the court also reaffirmed the rape myth that permits an acceptable aggressive standard of masculine conduct: the defendant—and men who exhibit similar behavior—"do not deserve such extreme penalties" as the felony rape charge.[97] Under this line of reasoning, the court further normalized notions of rough handling and violence as satisfactory forms of masculine seduction if there were no signs of struggle or injury. Specifically, "seduction" occurred when the female reluctantly consented because of his pressure.[98] Since visual marks such as scratches, bruises, or lacerations were not present, the court concluded that the victim might have been reluctant to have sex but eventually acquiesced under pressure—which was acceptable. Therefore, under this rationale, a man could still force sex on a "reluctant" victim who was not outwardly injured by his violence and hostility.

Goldberg v. State (1979) further reinforced acceptance of forced sex as a means of masculine seduction. In this case, the defendant lured the victim into an isolated building, as he posed as a modeling agent. When he made sexual advances toward her, the victim expressed her nonconsent, stating, "she didn't want to do that stuff."[99] However, she said that she felt helpless and scared of the defendant, since "he was so much bigger," and she was isolated "in a room

94 People v. Evans, 287 N.W. 2d 608, Mich. Ct. App. (1979).
95 *Id.*
96 *Id.* at 1091.
97 *Id.* at 1090.
98 *Id.*
99 *Goldberg v. State*, 395 A.2d. 1213, (1979).

alone with him" with no other buildings around.[100] In this case, the Maryland Court of Special Appeals insisted on a physical demonstration of either his force or threat of force and her nonconsent. The defendant's pushing her to the bed, her attempting to put her clothes back on, and her squeezing her legs shut to prevent penetration were not enough to demonstrate that he forced her.[101] The court mentioned that this testimony indicated the victim's reluctance to have sex with him, but not her resistance.[102] This reasoning shows that a male could still intimidate a woman and force sex upon her. If the victim did not put up too much of a fight, and if he cleverly orchestrated the circumstances so she could not prove force or threat of force, the perpetrator could compel sex on an unwilling female.[103]

Although both *Goldberg v. State* and *People v. Evans* are over 40 years old, the precedent these cases established still holds true in today's legal interpretation of consent, force, and threat of force. These cases indicate that to prove nonconsent, the female victim must place herself in further danger by resisting the rapist to the degree that she or he obtains injury—physical or ocular "proof" must be present for a rape charge. Following this reasoning in another case, in *Commonwealth v. Berkowitz* (1994), the court indicated that a victim's noninjurious self-defense measures were not enough to prove force or threat of force. In this instance, the victim stopped by a friend's dorm room while she was waiting for her boyfriend. Instead, she found the defendant who asked her to "hang out a while."[104] The defendant attempted to kiss the victim, who expressed nonconsent by saying "no."[105] However, he locked the door, pushed her to the bed, pinned her down by straddling her, and penetrated her. Throughout the encounter, the victim continued to object by saying "no," "I gotta go," and "let me go."[106] She explained that she could not physically resist because he was on top of her and she "couldn't go anywhere."[107]

Although the Pennsylvania Supreme Court found sufficient evidence to prove nonconsent, it found insufficient evidence to determine the state statute's requirement of "forcible compulsion" against her.[108] In other words, the

100 *Id.* at 60

101 *Id.* at 68.

102 *Id.*

103 One of the reasons prosecutors do not go forward with a rape case is due to pervasive rape myths such as that "real rape" involves a stranger who uses physical violence and a weapon and that "real victims" fight back. Morabito, Melissa S., Linda M. Williams and April Pattavina, *Decision Making in Sexual Assault Cases: Replication Research on Sexual Violence Case Attrition in the U.S.*, U.S. Department of Justice Office of Justice Programs' National Criminal Justice Reference Service. 75 (2019).

104 *Commonwealth v. Berkowitz*, 641 A.2d 1161 Pa. (1994).

105 *Id.* at 509.

106 *Id.*

107 *Id.* at 510.

108 *Id.* at 1164.

defendant's pinning her down and her inability to move were not enough to determine force or threat of force against her, and the court went on to suggest that the victim had several opportunities but "took no action against him."[109] For example, she could have put up a better fight when he pushed her to the bed and paused to untie her sweatpants, she could have attempted to run and unlock the door on several occasions, and she could have struggled more when he penetrated her.[110] This rationale suggests that a physically stronger male (which is often the case) can intimidate, strong arm, and have his way with a physically weaker woman. It also implies that the victim remains responsible for her own rape if she does not further place her life in a more dangerous predicament. In other words, "she asked for it."

The Fight, Flight, or Freeze Response

The problem with requiring a victim to put up a fight to show she was forced and did not consent is dangerous and impractical.[111] According to science, this reaction is oftentimes impossible, and studies have shown that most rape victims do not fight, yell, or attempt to run away. As psychologist and specialist of the neurobiology of trauma Dr. James W. Hopper puts it, "In the midst of sexual assault, the brain's fear circuitry dominates. The prefrontal cortex can be severely impaired, and all that's left may be reflexes and habits."[112] This reaction from the brain—commonly referred to as "trauma brain" —prepares the victim for the "fight or flight" response: "pupils dilate, hearing becomes more acute, and the pulse quickens. The victim is made ready for incoming attacks and avenues of escape."[113] However, although the brain prepares victims to better rely on their impulses and instincts during times of danger, many times victims neither fight nor flee. Instead, they freeze. Unlike soldiers in the military who have repetitively drilled and practiced "habit learning" techniques to rely upon during times of life-threatening stress, victims of sexual assault typically have no reflexes, habits, or impulses to help them

109 *Id.*

110 *Id.*

111 Norman B. Schmidt et al., *Exploring Human Freeze Responses to a Threat Stressor*, 39.3 J Behav Ther Exp Psychiatry, 292–293, 292 (Sept. 2008). Schmidt et al. argue that although the "fight or flight" response has been utilized since the 1920s, the medical community has not considered the "freeze" response as a more valid and more practical response in humans who have experienced trauma.

112 Jim Hopper, *Why Many Rape Victims Don't Fight or Yell*, The Washington Post (2015) https://www.jimhopper.com/pdfs/Hopper_WhyManyRapeVictimsDontFightorYell.pdf. See also Adrian W. Coxell and Michael B. King, *Adult Male Rape and Sexual Assault: Prevalence, Revictimization, and the Tonic Immobility Response*, in 25.4. Sexual & Relationship Therapy 372, 362 (Nov. 2010).

113 Hopper.

defend themselves.[114] Without such habits, these victims remain helpless, and they may completely freeze, experiencing what Dr. Hopper calls "tonic immobility."[115] Through tonic immobility, victims do not consciously "allow" themselves to be raped but instead become literally paralyzed with fear, and they are "unable to move, speak, or cry out."[116]

Yet without this better understanding of how the brain reacts during trauma, both law and the general public might initially assume that a victim who is under attack will scratch, claw, and kick her way out of being raped.[117] In the event that she does not react this way, it might be easy to assume that she consented to having sex when in fact, she was forced. In addition, there are a variety of responses that are dependent on the individual victim, her experiences, and her habits: "Most victims will freeze, if only briefly. Some will fight back, effectively. Some will resist in habitual, passive ways. Some will give in and cry. Others will become paralyzed, become faint, pass out, or disassociate."[118] Yet in most instances, the law relies on the false belief that if a victim is being attacked, she will fight back or try to get away; however, this is only one option among many. By making this assumption, the law neglects the most common responses: many victims will "freeze" when being faced with life-threatening trauma. As a result, the law neglects and dismisses a frequent response that could justify her nonconsent.[119]

The Freeze Response in *Thirteen Reasons Why*

In *Thirteen Reasons Why,* Hannah becomes angry with herself when she does not prevent Jessica from being sexually assaulted by Bryce. She admits she could "have stopped it," but she could not talk, and she could not move because her "mind [was] in meltdown."[120] In her state of helplessness, Hannah experienced another specific type of freeze response—the "detection freeze

114 *Id.*

115 *Id.*

116 *Id.*

117 According to Scaer, how victims react to traumatic stress has been misinterpreted by many communities and by society as a whole (xvi). He notes that the freeze response is an innate response that originates with prey animals in the wild but can also be seen in humans: "when prey animals are no longer able to flee or fight, they enter the freeze, or immobility, response" (xvii). Since human beings were once prey mammals, they still possess this type of response when they feel they have no means to escape life-threatening danger. ROBERT SCAER, THE BODY BEARS THE BURDEN: TRAUMA, DISASSOCIATION, AND DISEASE (2014).

118 Hopper, *Why Many Rape Victims Do Not Fight or Yell.*

119 Legal scholar, Catharine A. MacKinnon argues that the element of consent in rape cases should be broadened to include "disassociation," and "passivity and acquiescence." Catherine A. MacKinnon, *Rape Redefined*, HARVARD LAW AND POLICY REVIEW 447 (June 14, 2016).

120 ASHER at 226–267.

response."[121] This reaction occurs when something traumatic happens suddenly, and the onset of danger becomes instant and unrelenting. As a result, the event "massively escalates stress and the brain's defense circuitry not only detects the unexpected attack but automatically and involuntarily triggers strong brain and body responses."[122] In this instance, Bryce's entering the room and taking advantage of Jessica was completely unanticipated, and it happened quickly. Consequently, Hannah's detection freeze response resulted in "stopping all movement."[123] Emotionally fragile from months of being the victim of sexual harassment herself in addition to witnessing Jessica's rape, Hanna's prefrontal cortex attempted to protect her by shutting down and placing her in survival mode.

Shortly after witnessing Jessica's rape, Hannah's frail mental state and posttraumatic stress devolved into complete self-destruction. Irrational, she became even more consumed with guilt and self-loathing, and she could no longer trust her own decisions or actions. As Dr. Jim Hopper puts it, "like the brain of every survivor, every incident of sexual assault or severe sexual harassment is unique, and responses can unfold in unique and complex ways."[124] One way in which survivors of sexual trauma might cope is by attempting to dissociate through certain risk-taking behaviors.[125] Since the prefrontal cortex that controls decision-making, problem-solving, and advanced reasoning shuts down in survival mode, the victim is more prone to making unsafe or impulsive decisions. In this case, a few weeks after Jessica's rape, Hannah makes a reckless decision at another party when she decides to join Bryce alone in the hot tub. Although she knew Bryce was a rapist, she puts herself in harm's way, and she "did nothing to stop [him]."[126] When he began to place sexual advances on her, she did not verbally say "no," or "push [his] hand away."[127] Instead, she froze, clenching her jaw and attempting to hold back tears as he raped her.[128] Although passive, her body language still indicated that she did not want to have sex, and she did not consent. Although she blamed herself, Bryce had no right to rape her. Yet for Hannah, this ultimately became the last straw in the decision to end her own life: "I was done."[129]

121 Jim Hopper, *Freezing During Sexual Assault and Harassment*, Psychology Today (April 3, 2018) https://www.psychologytoday.com/us/blog/sexual-assault-and-the-brain/201804/freezing-during-sexual-assault-and-harassment

122 *Id.*

123 *Id.*

124 *Id.*

125 Jeffery W. Braunstein, *Post-Traumatic Stress Disorder in Rape Victims*, ResearchConsultation.com (2007) http://www.researchconsultation.com/InformationArticlesonMentalHealthProblems_05.asp

126 Asher at 263.

127 *Id.* at 264.

128 *Id.*

129 *Id.* at 266.

Feeling alone, ruined and without any means of help, support, or understanding, Hannah committed suicide shortly after Bryce raped her.

The Freeze Response and the Law

While both the criminal justice system and society at large have overlooked the complicated nature of trauma and a victim's "freeze response," the Supreme Court of California has considered certain reactions that do not fall under the guise of "fight" or "flight." For example, in *People v. Barnes* (1986), the court mentioned that some women experience "frozen fright" as a response to sexual assault.[130] Although this response might resemble cooperative behavior, "she may be in a state of terror" and "the victim may make submissive signs to her assailant and engage in propitiating behavior to inhibit further aggression."[131] Yet even though the court validated the freeze response in this case, the biggest issue was that the legislation that could have permitted the freeze response had been deleted in 1980. Unfortunately, it had been replaced by the statute that required a victim to struggle against the perpetrator to prove nonconsent—one that is commonly used in most states in the United States today.[132]

Nonetheless, the court in *People v. Barnes* explained that the older California statute prior to 1980 "defined rape as an act of sexual intercourse under circumstances where the person resists, but where 'resistance is overcome by force or violence' or where 'a person is prevented from resisting by threats of great and immediate bodily harm'."[133] Under the interpretation of this legislation, the victim should show signs of her resistance, but physical injuries were not required to prove nonconsent.[134] Consequently, the victim did not have to place herself in further danger by fighting off a perpetrator. Instead, "the amount of resistance needs[ed] only be such to manifest her refusal to consent."[135] Less narrowly construed by the courts and less dangerous for the victim, this type of resistance permitted a broader range of ways to

130 *People v. Barnes*, 42 Cal. 3d 284, Sup. Ct. Cal. (1986), 299.

131 Ibid.

132 In *People v. Iniguez* (1994), the Supreme Court of California explained that the legislation in 1980 allowed for different types of resistance within the "realm of personal choice" (853). By amending the statute to negate all types of resistance besides "fight," this "brought the law of rape into conformity with other crimes such as robbery, kidnapping and assault, which require force, fear, and non-consent to convict." (853). My view is that the crime of rape does not conform with these other crimes. Unlike the other crimes, the lines between sex, which is a noncriminal act, and rape, which is a criminal act, may be too easily manipulated by the strict requirements of the law. *People v. Iniguez*. 7 Cal.4th 847 (1994).

133 California Penal Code, § 261, subd. 3, (1980).

134 *People v. Barnes* at 293.

135 *Id.*

prove nonconsent. It allowed not only for the victim to fight or flee but it also reasoned why the victim would give up, give in, or freeze from inescapable fear and harm. Yet by removing these possibilities, the stricter legislation that courts employ today refuses to acknowledge these most common responses to trauma. As a result, this diminishes the possibility of proving nonconsent and the probability of punishing a guilty defendant by way of "proof beyond a reasonable doubt." As Carol E. Tracy puts it, narrowing the element of consent in this manner perpetuates a "biased perspective that continues to pervade the justice system's response to sex crimes."[136] This line of reasoning reinforces rape myths that focus on what women should do to prevent themselves from being raped instead of the criminal behavior and wrongdoing of the perpetrator himself.

Yet thanks to the #MeToo movement and the awareness it continues to raise, recently California broadened its legislation to reform how the state handles sex crimes. All this came to fruition after Brock Turner, the Stanford swimmer who was found raping an unconscious victim, served a punishment of only 6 months in prison and 3 years of probation.[137] After the judge's sentence sparked global outrage, legislators reformed the original statute that required physical force. In cases of unconscious victims under the old law, assailants like Turner could receive a lesser sentence upon the judge's discretion.[138] Yet after this incident, legislators eliminated the option for probation in these cases and broadened the definition of rape beyond the use of force or threat of force.[139] In addition, the state removed the statute of limitations for sex crimes.[140] Though the new laws do not consider the penultimate explanation of a conscious victim's "frozen fright" that rationalizes her inability to consent, California law makers recognize the need to change. Hopefully, these decisions will influence other states to consider the same.

Conclusion

The unique, nuanced ways in which survivors of sexual assault cope with and process trauma is clearly evinced in the example of Hannah Baker. In American law, the current strict standards to prove nonconsent most always

136 Carol E. Tracy et al., *Rape and Sexual Assault in the Legal System*, presented to National Research Council of the National Academies Panel on Measuring Rape and Sexual Assault in the Bureau of Justice Statistics Household Surveys Committee on National Statistics (June 5, 2012) https://sites.nationalacademies.org/cs/groups/dbassesite/documents/webpage/dbasse_080060.pdf

137 Matt Ford, *How Brock Turner Changed California's Rape Laws*, The Atlantic (Oct. 2016) https://www.theatlantic.com/news/archive/2016/10/california-law-brock-turner/502562/

138 *Id.*

139 *Id.*

140 *Id.*

fail the victim whom the law was designed to protect. Particularly in the cases of acquaintance rapes, perpetrators may easily rely on commonly accepted rape myths that shift blame to the victim, and both individual and institutional DARVO may occur. The study of both the law and *Thirteen Reasons Why* demonstrate the impracticality and danger a victim faces when the legal system requires her to "fight" against or "flee" from her stronger aggressor. The most reasonable and most common response—"freeze"—is unfairly ignored by both law and a culture of disbelief that blames the victim instead.

3 Domestic Violence

A Victim's Emotional Paralysis Mistaken for Acceptance in *Black and Blue* (1998)

In heterosexual relationships, intimate partner violence (IPV) is the most prevalent form of violence against women, and it is also the most poorly understood.[1] While we might think that the rate of the crime has decreased due to recent spikes in cultural awareness through the #MeToo movement, a current global study in *The Lancet* medical journal shockingly reveals that one in four women have experienced domestic abuse.[2] Like acquaintance rape, this form of violence is more normalized than an assault against a stranger due to the myth that the victim "lies," "consents," or somehow "accepts" the harm from their loved one.[3] In fact, "a significant number of Americans accept and even approve of family violence, with men more likely than women to excuse domestic abuse."[4] Consequently, compared to the cultural myths that suggest a sexual assault victim "asked for it," domestic violence victims face similar doubts. In this chapter, I acknowledge that multiple factors are involved in intimate partner violence. Problems arise due to police investigative procedures, family court limitations, and a lack of community resources in shelters and programs for women and children. Nonetheless, in this case, my focus remains on the prosecutorial process. Therefore, in this chapter, I argue that the criminal justice system should acknowledge a victim's "freeze" response from violence that ultimately leads to trauma. Most often, this trauma contributes to a victim's inaction to prosecute or her inability to leave the abuser.

1 Donna Scott Tilley, Susan M. Rugari, & Charles A. Walker, *Development of Violence in Men Who Batter Intimate Partners: A Case Study*, The Journal of Construction & Testing, 12.1.28, 28 (2008).

2 Lynnemaire Sardinha et al., *Global, Regional, and National Prevalence Estimates of Physical or Sexual, or Both, Intimate Partner Violence Against Women in 2018*, The Lancet, 339.1037. (Feb. 16, 2022). https://www.thelancet.com/journals/lancet/article/PIIS0140-6736(21)02664-7/fulltext

3 Reid Daitzman, *Domestic Violence Between Men and Women*, Psychology Today (Sept. 21, 2021), https://www.psychologytoday.com/us/blog/magical-enlightenment/202109/domestic-violence-between-men-and-women

4 Murray A. Straus, Richard J. Gelles, and Suzanne K. Steinmetz. Behind Closed Doors: Violence in the American Family 47 (1980). See Kersti Yllo and Murray A. Straus, *Interpersonal Violence Among Married and Cohabitating Couples*, 30 Fam. Rel. 339, 339 (1981): the public perceives marital violence as less serious than stranger violence.

DOI: 10.4324/9781003303572-3

While certainly some domestic abusers are women and some victims are men, for purposes of this chapter, the focus will be placed on the toxic, patriarchal influences that have historically permitted a male abuser to engage in violence toward his female partner. This abuser assumes the traditional role of "husband" or "caretaker," and his victim typically takes on the role of the "submissive" wife. For decades, the term "gender-based" violence has been created by legislation and interpreted through state and federal courts. Due to the overbearing number of female victims in domestic violence cases, in 1994 Congress created the Violence Against Women Act ("VAWA"), which contrived a legislative category of female victims and male abusers.[5] Backed by history and statistics, the law contextualized intimate partner violence around cis-heterosexual partners in a traditional husband/wife or male/female partnership due to the patriarchy that has reinforced such. However, that is not to say that this practice should continue as the norm. In fact, I recognize that this type of classification limits the disparities of different ethnic, racial, or socioeconomic classes of women and members of the LGBTQ+ community. Nevertheless, in this chapter, I analyze the patriarchal influences that not only dismiss the overwhelming number of victims in binary relationships but also exclude the exceptions to the rule.[6]

Black and Blue (1998)

With respect to cis-gender, heterosexual domestic violence, Anna Quindlen's *Black and Blue* (1998) is a story about a wife and mother, Francine Benedetto, who has been physically, mentally, and emotionally abused by her police officer husband, Bobby, for almost 20 years. One day after being severely bludgeoned and raped, she reaches the breaking point and decides to leave with her 10-year-old son, Robert. With the assistance of a network of people who help women get away from their abusive husbands, she leaves her home, nursing career, family, and friends. She becomes a new person, changing her name to Beth Crenshaw. Together with her son, they begin a new life far away from Brooklyn in Florida. Yet due to the posttraumatic stress disorder (PTSD) caused by long-term abuse, Beth is constantly looking over her shoulder in fear. She knows that Bobby—completely driven by anger and the need to control her—is looking for them, and he will never stop until he finds them. However, eventually, Beth becomes tired of the loneliness and fear of living

5 In 2013, the VAWA added protection to college students, immigrant and tribal women, and members of the LGBTQ community.

6 When exploring domestic violence within the same-sex LGBTQ community, "race, class, gender, sexuality and other social differences, moving beyond a simple gender lens to one involving a framework of intersectionality." Janice L. Ristock, Intimate Partner Violence in LGBTQ Lives 2, (2011).

in secret. As a result, she begins to let her guard down by confiding in a new friend, Mike Riordan. She also refuses to relocate after she is seen on the news during an incident at a carnival and after she learns that Robert made a phone call to his father because he misses him. So as predicted, Bobby finally catches up with them and finds her one night at her apartment. He chokes her until she passes out, and then he kidnaps Robert. The book ends with Beth trying to find Robert with the help of a private investigator, but they are unsuccessful. She marries Mike Riordan and has a child with him, but the audience is left feeling the helplessness of her inability to locate her son due to the lack of legal support and protection for her, a victim of domestic violence.

Domestic, Gendered Violence

Domestic violence occurs between domestic partners or spouses, and it revolves around intimacy, secrecy, shame, entrapment, and frustration within the space of the private home. Although the crime has decreased in the United States due to the VAWA (Violence Against Women Act) of 1994, a 2021 survey concluded that approximately 5.3 million women experience domestic violence each year.[7] According to the study, even though a number of victims consist of men, an overwhelming 85 percent of victims are women.[8] As a result, this survey, in addition to decades' worth of research, concludes that when domestic violence occurs, men most often abuse their female partners.[9] In this sense, I argue that domestic violence is primarily a gender-based, patriarchally influenced crime.[10] For the victims, intimate partner abuse is based upon traditional gender norms that reinforce an assumption that women are physically,

7 Amanda Kippert, *What is the Violence Against Women Act?* DomesticShelters.org (Nov.15, 2021), https://www.domesticshelters.org/articles/ending-domestic-violence/what-is-the-violence-against-women-act.

8 Kippert. See Kate Pickert, *What's Wrong with the Violence Against Women Act?* Time (Feb. 27, 2013): "VAWA has increased prosecution rates of domestic violence cases, but there is little conclusive evidence that it has significantly reduced the incidence of violence."

9 C.L. Yondis, *Gender Inequality, Violence Against Women, and Fear: A Cross-National Test of the Feminist Theory of Violence Against Women,* Journal of Interpersonal Violence 19 no. 6, 2004, at 655.

10 *Domestic Violence: Are Federal Programs Helping Curb the Abuse?* CQ Researcher, Nov. 15, 2013, 981, 983.; John Archer, *Sex Differences in Physically Aggressive Acts Between Heterosexual Partners: A Meta-Analytic Review,* Aggression and Violent Behavior, 7 no. 4, 2002, at 313.; Michael S. Kimmel, *"Gender Symmetry" in Domestic Violence,* Violence Against Women, 8 no. 11, 2002, at 1332.; R.E. Dobash and R.P. Dobash, *Domestic Violence: Sociological Perspectives,* International Encyclopedia of the Social and Behavioral Sciences 623–635, 2nd ed (2015). On the contrary, scholars of the "psychological supremacy" camp argue that gender constructs between masculinity and femininity should be removed since a minority of domestic abusers consist of women. Marianne Inéz Lien and Jørgen Lorentzen, Men's Experiences of Violence in Intimate Relationships loc. 403 (2019).

emotionally, and mentally inferior to men.[11] Under this rationale, a man may assume absolute control, authority, and dominance over the wife and any children who he feels are "beneath" him. To that end, the seclusion of the domestic space also contributes to the ease by which an abuser may resort to violence.[12]

Traditional Gender Norms and DARVO in *Black and Blue*

These abusers often possess a sense of hypermasculinity that reinforces aggressive masculine and passive feminine gender constructs.[13] A hypermasculine man typically believes that he should protect his honor, show courage, conceal fear, and resort to violence if needed to achieve these ideals.[14] These men also "fixate on the stereotyped sex roles that serve to maintain the double standard in our society: [a] virginal, loyal wife [and a] virile husband [who protects] his honor and property."[15] Under these circumstances, the husband may teach, chastise, and physically correct a wife if she gets out of line. In this case, she remains under the scrutiny of his dominant will and may rarely, if ever, voice her own opinions and autonomy. A hypermasculine male partner engages in toxic masculinity when he justifies or minimizes his mental, emotional, financial, or physical abuse toward his partner. Nonetheless, this form of violence rests not only with the abuser but also with his victim: both battered women and the batterers usually share the same traditional opinion about proper male and female roles.[16] For example, even if she works outside of the home, she believes that the true success of a woman depends on her wifely or motherly duties.[17] So in these instances, traditional views that identify women as submissive to men may reinforce masculine chastisement through violent measures.

These traditional gender norms of men and women in the household stem from patricentric influences that have dated back for centuries and have spanned across time periods, geographical locations, and cultural contexts. Of course, most men treat women and children in ethical, respectful ways; however, for some men, patriarchy gives them a sense of entitlement "to be completely and utterly in control [because they believe that] everything revolves around them."[18] Consequently, these men expect that everyone else in the family has "an absolute responsibility and obligation to keep them happy at all

11 Angela Hattery. The Social Dynamics of Domestic Violence 36 (2012).

12 Maggie Wykes and Kristy Welch. Violence, Gender, and Justice 7 (2009).

13 Del Martin. Battered Wives 62 (1977).

14 *Id.* at 62.

15 *Id.* at 62.

16 Kathleen Waits, *The Criminal Justice System's Response to Battering: Understanding the Problem, Forging the Solutions*, in Feminist Jurisprudence 188, 191 (Patricia Smith, ed., 1993).

17 Waits, at 191.

18 Jess Hill, See What You Made Me Do, 110 (2019).

times and do whatever it is they want."[19] A male of the household most often attempts to reinforce this notion through any measures necessary. This means that his abuse is not only physical but also psychological and emotional. With these tactics, in addition to limiting the woman's freedom and autonomy, he instils fear in her, and that fear is the reason why so many women remain in abusive relationships.[20]

One specific way in which many domestic and other interpersonal violence abusers instil fear and confusion is though the blame-shifting manipulation tactic called DARVO. An acronym coined by psychology professor Dr. Jennifer J. Freyd, DARVO stands for Deny, Attack, and Reverse Victim and Offender.[21] In *Black and Blue,* Bobby provides an example of DARVO when he first physically assaults Francine by grabbing her upper arm with such force that his fingertips bruised her like "a tattoo, a black sun with four small moons revolving around it."[22] The day after the assault, he denies it by minimizing his actions: "I didn't hit you. You know I didn't hit you."[23] He then shifts the blame by attacking Francine, instead: "You see, Fran, this is what you do."[24] Bobby then goes on to reverse the victim and offender: "You twist things. You always twist things."[25]

Like the first time Bobby manipulates Francine after the initial physical assault, he uses DARVO again when he abuses her for the last time after he finds her in Florida and almost kills her. He begins by denying his responsibility for the violence by blaming her instead: "You had everything you could want."[26] He then attacks her, "You took my son away from me. What, were you nuts?" and reverses victim and offender by explaining, "I loved you and look what you did to me."[27] By using DARVO, many male domestic abusers like Bobby assert their masculine power over what they consider the weaker, "lesser" female. In turn, they can both confuse and silence the victim and convince themselves that they are not accountable for any harm or wrongdoing. Because domestic violence occurs in private, DARVO and various forms of violence may easily become ongoing, normalized, and present in day-to-day life.

19 Hill, at 110.
20 Nicola Groves, Domestic Violence and Criminal Justice 10 (2011).
21 S. J. Harsey and Jennifer J. Freyd, *Deny, Attack and Reverse Victim and Offender (DARVO): What is the Influence on Perceived Perpetrator and Victim Credibility? In* 29 Journal of Aggression, Maltreatment, & Trauma, 897, 897 (2020).
22 Anna Quindlen, Black and Blue 5 (1998).
23 *Id.* at 6.
24 *Id.* at 5.
25 *Id.*
26 *Id.* at 270.
27 *Id.* at 275.

Archetypes for Domestic Abusers: Cobras and Pit Bulls

From the beginning in *Black and Blue* (1998), Anna Quindlen characterizes Bobby Benedetto with the traits of toxic masculinity. Moody, controlling, and an "alpha-male" who does not take no for an answer, Bobby's dynamic revolves around his ultimate power and authority and Beth's submission to it.[28] In a 1995 study, psychology professors John Gottman and Neil Jacobson discovered two distinct profiles for male domestic abusers like Bobby—what they called "Cobras" and "Pit Bulls"—in an attempt to determine why some men are more violent toward women.[29] In this case, they examined 200 couples' arguing styles and psychological responses such as heart rate, respiration, and blood pressure.[30] They found that while 80 percent of men experienced predictable responses such as increased heart rate and skyrocketed blood pressure, a surprising 20 percent showed the opposite.[31] For this group, as they became more aggressive toward their partners, their heart rates dropped.[32] The 80 percent majority group fell under the profile of the "Pit Bulls" who were co-dependent, extremely insecure, and perturbed with profound jealousy and paranoia.[33] In public, these abusers were typically described as "nice guys" because their "dark sides" and abusive nature would only surface in intimate relationships.[34] Relationships with "Pit Bulls" tended to be extremely volatile, and over half of the couples in the study had divorced after 2 years; however, none of the marriages had ended with women who were married to the minority 20 percent group called "Cobras" because, according to the research, these women were too terrified to leave.[35] Calm and calculating even in the heat of an aggressive argument, the "Cobras" maintained composure and could strike hard, fast, and unexpectedly.[36] The psychologists also found that these men possessed little interest in intimacy or emotional attachment and did not fear abandonment.[37] Statistically, many were most likely to have an antisocial personality disorder and suffered from severe childhood abuse or neglect.[38] Like Bobby Benedetto, the "Cobras" were hedonistic and entitled, and they abused their wives to get what they wanted.[39]

28 *Id.* at 5.

29 Gottman and Jacobson, When Men Batter Women: New Insights Into Ending Abusive Relationships 84 (2007).

30 *Id.*

31 *Id.*

32 *Id.*

33 *Id.* at 90, 92.

34 *Id.* at 38.

35 *Id.* at 30. The study found that violence of "Cobras" was typically more severe than that of "Pit Bulls." For example, 38 percent of "Cobras" had threatened their wives with weapons compared to only 4 percent of "Pit Bulls."

36 *Id.* at 84.

37 *Id.* at 84.

38 *Id.* at 93–96.

39 Quindlen, at 5.

Abusers Who Have Been Abused

Yet while both "Cobras" and "Pit Bulls" may appear violent and terrifying, this facade is actually an attempt to conceal deep-rooted feelings of fear and insecurity.[40] Probably angry and frustrated with their lives, these abusers may put up a strong front of control in public, but in the privacy of their homes, they cannot hide from feelings of inadequacy.[41] Although the explanation for domestic abuse is not an exact science, a perpetrator's feelings of insufficiency may arise from early childhood, especially since studies have shown that a good number of domestic abusers have been abused themselves.[42] While not all children become violent adults, many grew up in homes with rigid traditional gender roles, and their father harmed their mother.[43] So arguably for some of these men, the behavior was learned from such an early age that it became both a survival mechanism and a part of their own identity.

For example, Wendy Bunston explains that this "identity" of a domestically abused child begins in infancy.[44] Contrary to popular belief, infants and children are not "too young" to see, notice, or experience violence.[45] Unable to talk, crawl, or run away from danger, infants often "hide within themselves" when they realize that their caregivers expose them to and are unable to protect them from danger.[46] Thus the frightened infant's brain builds "restrictive pathways that serve the purpose of survival" in the amygdala, which processes fear.[47] Developing pathways of heightened awareness, this part of the brain responds to stimuli before the rational parts of it determine whether the threat is real or not.[48] As the child continues to grow up in a violent household, he learns to stay quiet and not to cry when he needs attention, which is opposite the reaction of a child in a nonabusive home.[49] By contrast, these children in violent homes understand that if they cry or complain, harm will ensue—as they have witnessed toward either them or their mother. Thus, as infants grow

40 Jana L. Jansinsky, *Theoretical Explanations for Violence Against Women*, in SOURCEBOOK ON VIOLENCE AGAINST WOMEN 5, 9 (Claire M. Rosetti, ed., 2013).

41 MARTIN, at 46.

42 Steven R. Tracy, *Abuse is Devastating*, MENDING THE SOUL (2021). https://mendingthesoul.org/resources/general/abuse-is-devastating/?gclid=CjwKCAiA9aKQBhBREiwAyGP5lUcgDLSdSpb7_hw6PCogRjUk9mz4bocZqNL_MpXQCVPF4dS-WIZy3hoC2foQAvD_BwE; QUINDLEN, at 6, 285. While they never directly speak of it, both Bobby and his mother imply that Bobby was severely abused by his father as a child.

43 It is estimated that about one-third of abused children will become abusers themselves. See Steven R. Tracy, *Abuse is Devastating*, MENDING THE SOUL (2021).

44 In JESS HILL, SEE WHAT YOU MADE ME DO 172 (2019).

45 HILL, at 172.

46 HILL, at 172.

47 WENDY BUNSTON AND ROBYN SKETCHLY, REFUGE FOR BABIES IN CRISIS: HOW CRISIS ACCOMMODATION SERVICES CAN ASSIST INFANTS AND THEIR MOTHERS AFFECTED BY FAMILY VIOLENCE 2 (2012).

48 HILL, at 182.

49 *Id.* at 182.

into children, they learn to repress their emotions, disassociate, and oftentimes blame themselves for their caregiver's abusive actions altogether.[50] In *Black and Blue*, Beth observed these characteristics in her young son Robert. She explains that his whole life revolved around witnessing abuse, and it "was eating the life out of him."[51] By the time he is 10 years old, Robert no longer asks about her injuries after altercations between her and Bobby. Instead, he "knew to be quiet, as though he thought this was the way life was."[52] Before her own eyes, her little boy "was becoming a dead man ... with a dead man's eyes."[53] This fact, in addition to the increased severity of Bobby's abuse, becomes the driving force behind the reason to finally leave her husband and to take her son with her.

Since abuse or neglect changes the brain functions and chemical structure, children also often have difficulty behaving, regulating emotions, or socially functioning.[54] Like Robert, these children may have been conditioned to be on "high alert" and hypersensitive to their environment. Many also have difficulty relaxing or they may experience anxiety. These characteristics combined with their repression of anger, frustration, or fear often contribute to the fact that many children who have been abused may repeat what they experienced as a child in their adult lives.[55] As Dr. Reid J. Daitzman puts it, "often the abuser was abused by their family of origin, had poor role models who settled conflict through aggression, [and] has a low frustration tolerance."[56]

Substance Abuse and Abusers

Although profiles of certain male abusers may be categorized as either "Pit Bulls" or "Cobras," all of them typically possess many of the same characteristics. As Del Martin explains, most are "alcoholics, psychotics, or plain and simple bullies."[57] In the case of Bobby Benedetto, he embodies all three: in addition to his hyperaggressive nature and antisocial personality, Bobby consumes alcohol on a regular basis, using the substance as a coping mechanism

50 *Id.*

51 QUINDLEN, at 21.

52 *Id.*

53 *Id.*

54 Leonard Holmes, *How Emotional Abuse in Childhood Changes the Brain,* VERY WELL MIND (Nov. 15, 2021), https://www.verywellmind.com/childhood-abuse-changes-the-brain-2330401.

55 Steven R. Tracy, *Abuse is Devastating,* MENDING THE SOUL, (2021): "Recent neurological research has definitely shown that early childhood abuse, neglect, and witnessing family violence permanently alters and damages the brain, thus leading to a host of long-term individual and social pathologies."

56 Reid J. Daitzman, *Domestic Violence Between Men and Women.* PSYCHOLOGY TODAY, (Sept. 2021). https://www.psychologytoday.com/us/blog/magical-enlightenment/202109/domestic-violence-between-men-and-women

57 MARTIN, at 49.

to hide from his own insecurities, negative feelings, difficult memories, and character flaws. Some violent domestic abusers like Bobby use alcohol to avoid processing problematic emotions and to temporarily "escape" from reality. Yet simultaneously, alcohol lowers inhibitions and adds fuel to anger and aggression. Out of convenience, abusers can then use their intoxication as an "excuse" for losing their temper or for "forgetting" violent exchanges that might have happened the night before. In fact, Beth immediately associates Bobby's alcohol use with danger, to the point where she "was afraid of having booze in the house."[58] Yet while alcohol and substance abuse may exacerbate an abuser's volatility, cruelty, and lack of inhibitions, it is important to note that addiction neither causes nor cures his reason to hurt his spouse.[59] While some may attempt to explain away or excuse their aggression due to alcohol or drug use, most violent men who recover from addiction continue to abuse.[60] Ultimately, the reason why they abuse is much more psychologically complex than being due to insobriety.

Victimology: Why He Chooses Her

According to concepts of victimology, abusers choose victims who they consider submissive, meek, or "weak"—someone who is least likely to put up a fight. Either consciously or unconsciously, domestic abusers tend to select and groom victims with certain passive characteristics that are in stark contrast to their own aggressive tendencies. In the case of Bobby and Beth's courtship in their early 20's, Bobby is described as charismatic, popular, and handsome while Beth is a quiet, self-conscious introvert. Either intentionally or unintentionally, Bobby picks up on Beth's passivity as a good "match" for his own intimidation and cruelty. Since Beth views herself as someone who was never "special" in any way, she immediately falls hard for Bobby who showers her with his affections.[61] Unlike Beth, Bobby the attention-seeker is always surrounded by numerous friends who listen to him and laugh at his jokes, and his mother completely dotes on her only child. From the beginning, Beth idealizes the hypermasculine, police officer Bobby and views him as a man who takes charge and provides for his family—which is the opposite of her own neglectful, passive father.[62] Beth also comes from a childhood of poverty and instability, and one of the main reasons it takes her so long to leave

58 Quindlen, at 146.

59 Lundy Bancroft, Why Does He Do That?: Inside the Minds of Angry and Controlling Men 191 (2002).

60 *Id.*

61 Quindlen, at 53.

62 Quindlen, at 21.

Bobby is because she fears going back "there" to the life of her past.[63] In addition, she loves Bobby and his intensity, and even though he begins to isolate her from friends and family and starts to physically abuse her before they get married, she hopes that the abuse is only temporary. She believes things will get better, but instead it only gets worse.[64]

Toxic Love and the Cycle of Domestic Violence

One of the most complex concepts of domestic violence is that despite the physical and psychological harm, victims like Beth love the abuser.[65] The relationship does not start with abuse. It begins gradually and after the victim has fallen in love. For those who have been groomed, they come to believe that love is jealous, chaotic, hurtful, and extreme. Beth confuses Bobby's intense feelings for her that start with verbal insults and later resort to physical violence as "love." This idea of romantic love being painful and difficult is nothing new, as the concept is romanticized in the media, film and entertainment industry, and society in general. In addition, many of us have been conditioned as children to believe that love hurts, to some degree. For example, bel hooks explains that the "majority of us" were brought up in dysfunctional families where we were shamed or verbally or physically abused.[66] We learned that we were not "okay" as we were. We were taught that being abused or neglected was part of what it means to be cared for within a family unit.[67] Thus, "many of us cling to a notion of love that either makes abuse acceptable or at least makes it seem that whatever happened was not that bad."[68] "Toxic love," then translates to "love" in general for many of us, and Beth Benedetto provides an extreme example of this concept.

In addition, M. Scott Peck explains that part of what makes us humans relies on using feelings or emotion to lead us into romantic love relationships, despite the red flags and regardless of whether one person is a strong, compatible match to the other.[69] This idea corresponds to the common saying, "love is blind." In other words, many of us rely on our emotions instead of our sense of reason when it comes to choosing a partner. Based on attraction for someone else, this concept of emotional attachment is called "cathexis," and

63 *Id.* at 167.
64 *Id.* at 10–12.
65 *Id.* at 110.
66 BEL HOOKS, ALL ABOUT LOVE: NEW VISIONS 6 (2001).
67 *Id.*
68 HOOKS, at 6.
69 M. SCOTT PECK, MD, THE ROAD LESS TRAVELED: A NEW PSYCHOLOGY OF LOVE, TRADITIONAL VALUES, AND SPIRITUAL GROWTH 94 (25th Anniversary ed. 2002).

it is oftentimes confused with real love.[70] Yet cathexis is the opposite of true love. Rather, it is a self-serving form of connection to a person, place, or thing in the hopes that the outside object will fulfil an emotional need. In domestic violence situations, this form of emotional attachment may be used to insist that a person "loves" someone even if they are being hurt or neglected by the other partner.[71]

In the case of Beth and Bobby, part of their toxic relationship revolves around a cycle of repentance that occurs after he abuses her.[72] His extreme reaction and contrition serves to confuse her into thinking he "loves" her when in fact he only uses her for his own narcissistic purposes. In other words, he sets her up for more violence, and with each cycle, he can further shift the blame and manipulate her on a deeper level.[73] As years go by, he chips away at her self-confidence. He verbally denigrates her, and she feels like a "slut" and a "whore."[74] He also gaslights her, causing her to doubt herself and even question her own sanity.[75] Over time, a routine of order, love, and fear becomes normalized in their home.[76] Even as the abuse and danger increase, Beth still loves the idea of him, despite the fact that she fears him more and more.[77] As his unpredictable mood swings keep her on edge, she walks on eggshells and never knows what will set him off.

This heightened sense of awareness, while harmful, may be considered "exciting" in a way. In fact, like alcohol or drug dependency, an abusive relationship may become physically or psychologically addictive. For example, when the body is stressed by the chaos and violence, the brain releases high levels of the stress hormone, cortisol.[78] When the cycle of reward or affection follows the abuse, the brain then releases dopamine.[79] Therefore, the brain and body are continually prepped for danger then recover from the momentary release of it only to repeat the cycle over again. As psychotherapist Willow Smith puts it, "While drugs produce intense euphoria rewiring the brain for addiction instead of healthier activities, an individual in an emotionally abusive relationship may desperately seek the pleasurable connection they

70 *Id.* at 94.
71 Hooks, at 5.
72 Quindlen, at 72.
73 *Id.* at 270, 292.
74 *Id.* at 18.
75 *Id.* at 5.
76 *Id.* at 167.
77 *Id.* at 99, 21.
78 Lindsay Dodgson, *People Often Stay in Abusive Relationships Because of Something Called 'Trauma Bonding'—Here Are the Signs It's Happening to You*, Insider (Aug. 17, 2017 at 5:46 AM), https://www.businessinsider.com/trauma-bonding-explains-why-people-often-stay-in-abusive-relationships-2017-8
79 Dodgson.

experienced intermittently with their abuser."[80] When this way of life and "toxic love" becomes normalized for victims, the safety and trustworthiness of healthy love may seem foreign, and even boring. As a result, victims often acquire a misrepresented version of what real, healthy love should look like, and abusers continue to abuse because of this distortion.

How the Law Fails Victims

Due to socially acceptable forms of toxic love and patriarchal norms that reinforce gender roles of a man's superiority over a woman's, the criminal justice system most often fails victims of violence against women. An adversarial institution that views everything in black or white, guilt versus innocence, and victim versus defendant, it leaves very little room for compromise. The criminal justice system is also not favorable to the realities, nuances, and complications of "real" life—which is anything but black and white. For example, despite a victim's injuries, a prosecutor must bear the burden of proving an offender's guilt, and defense attorneys "manipulate facts in the name of zealous advocacy, and 'expert' witnesses obscure the truth."[81] It is also a skewed system where statistics are influenced by success rates. These success rates depend on both a judge's number of trials and a prosecutor's percentage of convictions.[82] Yet perhaps most importantly, despite over twenty years of reform, "there are still judges on the bench who…[remain] ignorant of the dynamics of abuse, abuse their own power, or engage in overt sexism."[83] And even when judges do not explicitly participate in these forms of behavior, many consider cases and make their decisions based on biased stereotypes of battered women who are "weak, helpless, and psychologically disturbed."[84] By immediately questioning victims' decisions and credibility, these judges view them under a lens of suspicion and disbelief, and they either consciously or unconsciously favor the offender. Such sexist stereotypes continue to

80 In Syeda Saad, *My Therapist Told Me to Treat My Emotionally Abusive Relationship Like the Addiction It Is*, Pop Sugar (Dec. 3, 2020). https://www.popsugar.com/love/why-emotionally-abusive-relationships-are-like-addiction-48018433

81 Michelle Kaminsky, Reflections of a Domestic Violence Prosecutor: Suggestions for Reform 10 (2012).

82 *Id.* at 10.

83 *Id.* at 11; See also Julie M. Kafka, *Judging Domestic Violence From the Bench: A Narrative Analysis of Judicial Anecdotes About Domestic Violence Protective Orders.*, Qualitative Health Research 29(8) 2019, at 1132, 1132: "judges may still endorse DV myths or stereotypes at a subconscious level, resulting in judicial behaviors that inadvertently undermine survivors."

84 Kaminsky, at 11; See also Jacqueline Clarke, *(In)Equitable Relief: How Judicial Misconceptions About Domestic Violence Prevent Victims From Attaining Innocent Spouse Relief Under I.R.C. § 6015(F)*, 22 Am. U. J. Gender Soc. Pol'y & L. 825, 825 (2013–2014).

influence both legal institutions and personnel, which in turn, undermine the legal system's aspiration to combat the abuse.[85]

Even in situations where an assailant has been officially charged with domestic violence, many prosecutorial proceedings limit a conviction, and acquittal or minimal punishment favors the defendant. Similar to how rapists can easily get away with sexual assault, domestic abusers can then acquire a "hitting license" when the criminal justice system's response fails to adequately punish them.[86] Law enforcement and legal intervention prove problematic since abuse occurs within the intimate sphere of the family space as opposed to a public one. Even when police are called during an acute beating session and they arrest the aggressor, the batterer is not usually convicted. Ultimately, the charge may be dropped or reduced to a lesser offense. In cases where the aggressor is charged, a pre-trial diversion—which is part of the plea-bargaining process—reduces the sentence.[87] Under this agreement, the conviction is suspended so long as the wrongdoer complies with the terms of the agreement. These terms may include abiding by a protective order, participating in counseling, undergoing a treatment program, or completing community service. In the rare instances when a defendant is convicted of the crime, he is more than likely assigned to probation instead of incarceration.[88] Overemphasizing family unity or a victim's lack of participation, many judges have become "unduly reluctant" to sentence domestic abusers to jail.[89] Like acquaintance rape cases, unless the violence consists of a felonious aggravated assault or unless another crime occurred in addition to the assault, the current legal system tends to withdraw from rigorous punitive measures.

Another factor that comes into play includes a reluctant victim who does not wish to testify against her spouse. In most cases, victims rarely want to prosecute because they do not want their spouse to serve time. Instead, they want him to get help, correct his behavior, and to stop mistreating them.[90] Like Beth Benedetto, most victims still love their abusers and simply want him to change. Consequently, the abused, the abuser, and the legal system contribute to the idea of an acceptable form of violence that revolves around traditional gender roles and conventional concepts of family.

85 Deborah Epstein and Lisa A. Goodman, *Discounting Women: Doubting Domestic Violence Survivors' Credibility and Dismissing Their Experiences,* 167 U. PA. L. REV. 399, 399 (2018–2019); Kathleen Waits, *The Criminal Justice System's Response to Battering: Understanding the Problem, Forging the Solutions,* FEMINIST JURISPRUDENCE 188, 188 (Patricia Smith, ed. 1993).

86 Waits, at 188.

87 Claire Dalton and Elizabeth M. Schneider, *The Criminal Justice System* IN BATTERED WOMEN AND THE LAW, 564, 575 (2001).

88 *Id.* at 576.

89 *Id.* at 205.

90 KAMINSKY, at 12.

History of Domestic Violence and the Law: The Doctrine of Chastisement

That concept of masculine authority and control of the domestic space traces back to the English Renaissance time period and perhaps even earlier. Deborah S. Cosimo argues that the history of domestic violence has its roots in the English common law doctrine of chastisement.[91] Reinforcing the notion of masculine control, the male "head" could physically "chastise," "correct," or punish women, children, and servants in order to ensure domestic order.[92] Under the "rule of thumb," a husband could beat his wife "with a stick no larger than a thumb."[93] So a husband could physically punish his wife as long as he did not excessively beat, bruise, maim, wound, or kill her. However, the doctrine promoted indiscriminate violence since physical punishment occurred within the intimacy of the home, and the man was given broad latitude. Although physical correction was permissible during the colonial time period in the US, in 1641 Puritans in the Massachusetts Bay Colony ordained the *Body of Liberties* that criminalized physical domestic abuse: "Everie marryed woeman shall be free from bodilie correction or stripes by her husband, unlesse it be in his owne defence upon her assault."[94] However the *Body of Liberties* was rarely enforced, and it existed only as a symbolic law.[95] To that end, the US appropriated the doctrine of chastisement that was upheld from 1750 to the early 1800s, and it rested on strong cultural beliefs that enforced masculine authority in the home.[96]

Affirming the idea of order through physical correction, the US courts established precedent for the doctrine of chastisement through three state court rulings during the 1800s in Mississippi and North Carolina: *Bradley v. State* (1824), *State v. Black* (1864), and *State v. Rhodes* (1868). Following "ancient common law" traditions, the court in *Bradley v. State* (1824) confirmed that a man may "chastise" his wife and use "salutary restraints in every case of [his wife's] misbehavior."[97] Under this pretext, the court explained that a husband may use physical force against his wife when she requires "moderate correction" because he remains responsible for her conduct.[98] In this particular case where Calvin Bradley beat and visibly bruised his wife, the

91 Deborah S. Cosimo, Domestic Violence and Recidivism Rates Among Male Perpetrators 8 (2012).

92 Susan Dwyer Amussen, *Punishment, Discipline, and Power: The Social Meanings of Violence in Early Modern England*, 6 Journal of Brit. Studies 1, 4–5 (1995).

93 Susan Dwyer Amussen, *'Being Stirred to Much Quietness': Violence and Domestic Violence in Early Modern England*, 6 Journal of Women's Hist. 70, 74 (1994).

94 William H. Whitmore, The Body of Liberties 51 (1890).

95 Cosimo, at 8.

96 Cosimo, at 9.

97 *Calvin Bradley v. The State*, Supp. Ct. Miss, 156, 156 (1824).

98 *Bradley v. The State*, at 156.

court determined that his acts of chastisement were acceptable, and the court reinforced the "rule of thumb:" he could punish her with weapons such as a "a whip or rattan, [that were] no bigger than his thumb."[99]

State v. Black (1864) affirmed and advanced the Mississippi Supreme Court's ruling in that "a husband cannot be convicted of a battery on his wife unless he inflicts a permanent injury or uses such excessive violence or cruelty as indicates malignity or vindictiveness."[100] In this case, Jesse Black accused his wife of infidelity, seized her by the hair, and forced and held her to the ground.[101] Such force was considered an acceptable, nonexcessive means of correction. The North Carolina court stated that since she started the argument, he became enraged "in a passion" and was provoked by her "excessive abuse."[102] In other words, the court blamed her for evoking his anger that led to him injuring her. Moreover, the court stated that a husband could take physical measures against his wife to correct and control her bad behavior.[103] In doing so, the *Black* court substantiated an avoidant attitude toward domestic disputes. Reinforcing masculine authority, the *Black* court explained that the law should leave the parties to themselves, "as the best mode of inducing them to make the matter up and live together as man and wife should."[104]

State v. Rhodes (1868) agreed with the *Black* court's judgment of non-interference. It determined that physical domestic violence existed as "trifles" in the home that lacked the legitimacy of a true assault.[105] The court explained that although a husband did not have a right to beat and seriously injure his wife, the court would not intervene since these types of punishments occurred within the domestic space.[106] Emphasizing the husband's authority in the home, the court minimized abuse: a husband's physical corrections were acceptable since "affection [between spouses] will soon forget and forgive."[107] As a result of not only the *Rhodes* but also the *Bradley* and *Black* rulings, men could physically punish their wives so long as they avoided permanently injuring them, and these factors remained in place in the US until the 1970s.[108] Ultimately, these cases permitted an "honor" system that allowed men to abuse women in their household.

99 *Id.* at 157.
100 *State v. Jesse Black*, 60 N.C. 266 Supp. Ct. N.C. (Raleigh 1864).
101 *Id.*
102 *Id.*
103 *Id.*
104 *Id.*
105 *State v. A.B. Rhodes*, 61 Supp. Ct. N.C. 453 (1868).
106 *Id.* at 453.
107 *Id.* at 457.
108 Barbara Mantell, *Domestic Violence*, in CQ RESEARCHER, Nov. 15 2013 at 982, 991.

Domestic Violence Law in Modern Times

Although modern US law has since taken measures to curb abuse against female domestic violence victims, the longstanding notion of masculine control through physical correction has complicated the enforcement of reform legislation. A new level of social concern arose at the turn of the twentieth century, and family courts were created.[109] These courts specialized in domestic violence and highlighted the criminality of it.[110] Nevertheless, enforcement was rarely effective.[111] For example, although family court judges believed they were helping to reduce abuse, discourage divorce, and urge reconciliation, women would most often return home and receive a beating for having filed a public complaint against their husbands.[112] To that end, reform efforts did not arise again until the 1970s when women's consciousness groups began to establish shelters for battered women.

Since around that time, Congress has carried out domestic violence reform measures through federal legislation such as the Victims of Crime Act (1984), the Family Violence Prevention and Services Act (1994), and the Violence Against Women Act (1994, 2000, 2005, 2013). Through these laws and others, state and federal funding contributes to domestic violence counseling and shelters. For example, the Victims of Crime Act in the mid-1980s allowed states to issue warrantless arrests without requiring an officer to witness a crime.[113] Media coverage also slowly acknowledged domestic violence in the 1990s and captured the public's attention. In 1994, the famous OJ Simpson case increased awareness of the seriousness of the crime when Simpson was charged with murdering his ex-wife, Nicole Brown Simpson, and her friend, Ronald Goldman. Simpson had been previously arrested for domestic violence, and the trial prosecutors uncovered evidence of his past repeated assaults, threats, obsessive jealousy, and stalking of Ms. Simpson.[114] Due to the notoriety of the Simpson case, Congress passed the Violence Against Women Act (VAWA) in 1994.[115] In 2013, the VAWA has been renewed and extended to protect Native Americans, gay, bisexual, and transgender victims of domestic.[116]

Coinciding with increased public awareness that started in the 1970's, the courts began to acknowledge gender-based violence in cases where physical abuse was evident. In the North Carolina Supreme Court case, *State v. Gurganus*

109 *Id.* at 993.
110 *Id.*
111 *Id.*
112 *Id.* at 993.
113 *Id.* at 994.
114 Evan Stark, Coercive Control: How Men Entrap Women in Personal Life 3 (2009).
115 Mantell, at 996.
116 *Id.*

(1979) the defendant alleged a violation of his Fourteenth Amendment Equal Protection rights that arose from a state statute which enhanced the punishment for men who assault women.[117] The defendant claimed that the statute violated his rights due to an unlawful gender-biased classification or "reverse discrimination."[118] Nonetheless, the Supreme Court of North Carolina upheld the state statute and did not find error in the trial court or appellate court rulings. The court focused on the unequal physical advantage of men over women: "We base our decision…upon the demonstrable and observable fact that the average adult male is taller, heavier and possesses greater body strength than the average female."[119] Although the court confirmed the need for gender equality in "equal employment opportunity, participation in sports and other areas," the reasoning ended with physical strength.[120] The court concluded that "larger and stronger males are likely to cause greater physical injury" to smaller females.[121] In this sense, the court recognized gender-based domestic violence and attempted to deter it by focusing on a man's size and physical advantage as rationale for an enhanced punishment.

It was not until almost twenty years later and after the federal government passed the 1994 Violence Against Women Act that the courts began to broaden the scope of the definition of domestic violence and consider other factors besides just physical abuse. For example, *Cesare v. Cesare* (1998) illustrates how courts in the 1990s began to consider "terroristic threats" and "harassment" as additional forms of abuse. Reflecting upon the helplessness of women who were abused in the home, the New Jersey court explained that domestic violence victims received "different treatment from similar crimes when they occur[ed] in a domestic context."[122] Furthermore, the court recognized the victims' "substantial difficulty in gaining access to protection from the judicial system, particularly due to that system's inability to generate a prompt response in an emergency situation."[123] As a result, abused and battered women "were not adequately protected by the police, the courts, or society as a whole."[124]

The court justified this reasoning in the case where Mrs. Cesare was subject to Mr. Cesare's violent threats over the course of several months. Mr. Cesare's threats included tying her to the railroad tracks near the back of their home, locking her in their backyard shed and causing a propane explosion, hiring a contract killer to murder her, and finally, shooting her with guns

117 *State v. Gurganus*, 250 S.E.2d, 668 Supp. Ct. N.C. 670 (1971).
118 *Id.* at 670.
119 *Id.* at 671.
120 *Id.*
121 *Id.*
122 *Cesare v. Cesare*, 713 A.2d 390, 391 (1998).
123 *Id.* at 391.
124 *Id.*

kept in their home.[125] Under these circumstances, the court determined that his actions and words consisted of "terroristic threats" that carried a "serious promise of death."[126] Considering that an ordinary, reasonable person would have felt the same as Mrs. Cesare, the court decided that Mr. Cesare seriously threatened her life. Although Mrs. Cesare did not suffer physical assault or injury, the court explained the complex nature of domestic violence, and it affirmed the position to take all domestic threats seriously.[127] Nonetheless, although the *Cesare* court recognized the need to consider more than physical abuse, the court limited the scope of mental abuse only to threats without considering intimidation, isolation, and control.

The Most Common Form of Domestic Abuse: Coercive Control

Even today, legislation and court opinion limit domestic abuse only to physical force or threats and dismiss other forms of harm. For example, the Texas Family Code mirrors most state statutes in defining "Family Violence" as "an act by a member of a family or household against another member of the family or household that is intended to result in physical harm, bodily injury, assault, or sexual assault or that is a threat that reasonably places the member in fear of imminent physical harm, bodily injury, assault, or sexual assault, but does not include defensive measures to protect oneself."[128] In this case, the Family Code statute restricts the definition only to bodily harm or a threat of bodily harm. However, many other forms of abuse arise and are often more prevalent in domestic violence cases.

Therefore, one solution is to broaden statutory definitions to include "coercive control." This would help identify and punish abusers who engage in psychological control measures.[129] Coercive control, which remains marginal to mainstream thinking, exists as the most common form of domestic abuse, and the enforcer subjects the victim to multiple control tactics.[130] Examples include the denial of money, the monitoring of time, stalking, isolation, and the restriction of mobility and communication.[131] Coercive control "disables a woman's capacity to effectively resist or escape abuse, a condition referred to as 'entrapment.'"[132] Due to a victim's isolation in addition to the lack of

125 *Id.* at 396.
126 *Id.* at 393.
127 *Id.* at 391.
128 Tex. Fam. Code § 71.004 (2017).
129 Stark, Coercive Control at 12.
130 *Id.*
131 *Id.* at 13.
132 Evan Stark, *Current Controversies: Coercive Control*, in Domestic Violence Law 48, 48 (Nancy K.D. Lemon, ed. 2018).

support and resources, coercive control instils fear. Therefore, while we might think that victims dread physical abuse the most, coercive control creates the worst damage.[133] An "invisible" strategy, it compares to "brainwashing and other coercive persuasion tactics used with hostages, prisoners of war, kidnap victims, and pimps with prostitutes."[134]

To that end, Scotland and Canada now define violence against women from a "human rights perspective" that includes coercive and controlling behaviors in addition to physical assault.[135] By contrast, the US maintains its traditional, more restrictive definition that only includes physical force or threat of force. However, since several domestic violence studies indicate that an abuser employs coercive control 80 percent of the time, the US should also extend the definition of family violence to include isolation, deprivation, and intimidation.[136] With these measures, the US could better protect domestic violence victims.

The Reluctant Victim and Evidence-Based Prosecution

Yet even if the US were to enhance its legislation, prosecuting domestic violence cases might still prove problematic because of the complexity of how law, society, and victims view the crime and minimize its seriousness. Specifically, many victims feel reluctant and sometimes refuse to proceed with the case because they fear their abuser will retaliate with even more abuse, especially with covert coercive control tactics.[137] In response to such cases, many jurisdictions began implementing evidence-based prosecutions in which the victim's testimony does not exist as the sole or primary source of evidence. Nonetheless, without the victim's corroborating testimony, the evidentiary strength of the case becomes significantly diminished, and the case most often favors the defendant's acquittal. Portraying the complexities of victim reluctance, *People v. Brown* (2001) discloses the difficulty of evidence-based prosecution without the cooperation of the victim. Without her full commitment to testify against her husband in the domestic violence incident, the court imposed a lesser punishment.

In *People v. Brown* (2001), the defendant and football star Jim Brown was accused of abusing his wife. He was charged with two misdemeanors--terroristic threat and vandalism--but the jury only convicted him of vandalism, a lesser offense. Mr. Brown rejected his sentence for vandalism that included

133 Stark, Coercive Control at 12.

134 *Id.*

135 *Id.* at 13.

136 *Id.*

137 Elizabeth M. Schneider, et al. Domestic Violence and the Law: Theory and Practice, 315 (2d. ed. 2008).

probationary terms, and he appealed the sentencing terms to the California appellate and superior court. Arguing abuse of discretion of the trial court, he stated that the trial court imposed "unauthorized" and "illegal" probationary terms.[138] However, the superior court agreed with the trial court's punishment. Consequently, Mr. Brown opted to serve jail time. So, although he was punished under the vandalism charge, the jury acquitted him on the terroristic threat charge. The main reason for the acquittal was because his wife—the victim—refused to testify against him. This then diminished both his wrongful conduct and the seriousness of the offense.

In this case, the police responded to Monique Brown's 911 call. The officers stated that upon their arrival, Mrs. Brown appeared visibly upset, stating that she and the defendant were involved in a heated argument over his infidelity.[139] Indicating that a direct terroristic threat occurred, she told the officers that Mr. Brown stated that "he was going to kill her by snapping her neck," and he followed her out of the house and into the garage.[140] In the garage, he repeatedly struck her vehicle with a shovel and "busted out" the windows.[141] In her statement, she also recounted a history of his physical abuse during their two-year marriage that she never reported.[142] According to the officers, when Mrs. Brown disclosed this information, she appeared of sound mind and "did not seem reluctant to discuss these matters."[143]

Nonetheless, when she testified at trial, she dramatically changed her story, and her testimony helped exonerate Mr. Brown of the domestic terroristic threat charge. Compared to her initial report, she stated that Mr. Brown had never threatened her, and she never felt that she was in danger.[144] Diminishing Mr. Brown's responsibility, she mentioned that he suffered from deep depression and grief over the recent death of his best friend.[145] She also shifted blame for Mr. Brown's actions onto herself. She stated that she had antagonized him with accusations of infidelity, and she broke the lamp and glasses that were found in their home at the time of his arrest.[146] Admitting that she attempted to provoke him, she explained that she had been out with a male friend, knowing it would upset him.[147] Further contradicting the initial police report, she also testified that there had never been any other incidents

138 *People v. Brown*, 117 Cal. Rptr. 2d 738, 746 (2001).
139 *Id.* at 739.
140 *Id.* at 739.
141 *Id.* at 740.
142 *Id.* at 739.
143 *Id.* at 740.
144 *Id.* at 743.
145 *Id.* at 741.
146 *Id.* at 742, 744.
147 *Id.* at 741.

of domestic violence.[148] By diminishing Mr. Brown's accountability for his actions, Mrs. Brown legitimized her husband's violence and minimized his chances of criminal punishment.

Monique Brown's confounding trial testimony abated the probative value of her statements in the initial police report. In this sense, by indicating that she had lied, Mrs. Brown impeached herself and thwarted her own credibility. As a result, the jury exonerated Mr. Brown of the terroristic threat charge, thereby shifting the "guilt" from him—the abuser—to her—the victim. In addition, a licensed psychiatrist, who was the expert witness, successfully blamed Mrs. Brown for provoking his hostility. Helene MacDonald, the expert witness, testified that Mrs. Brown suffered from Borderline Personality Disorder (BPD). She stated that Ms. Brown's BPD caused her to "make [Mr. Brown] angry and jealous" since she could not tolerate the feelings of abandonment and rejection as he withdrew in grief over his friend.[149] Ms. MacDonald's testimony combined with Mrs. Brown's self-reproach during trial helped negate the charge of terroristic threat and confirm how the perception of others may also reinforce domestic violence against women. Explaining the paradoxes within the criminal justice system and the reasoning behind her reluctance, Linda Mills explains: "Mrs. Brown had two options: she could protect herself by testifying against her husband, or she could protect her husband by not testifying against him. Mrs. Brown made the decision that most women make: she chose to protect her husband."[150] By her doing so, however, the trial expert was also was able to successfully shift blame away from Mr. Brown. Ultimately, this case shows both the difficulty a wife experiences and the ease by which domestic assault may be diminished through the law.

Battered Woman Syndrome, Learned Helplessness, and the Freeze Response

Another reason why prosecuting domestic violence cases proves difficult is due to the to the complicated predicament of battered women, in general. Criminal law first adopted the term "battered woman" in the New Jersey Supreme Court landmark case, *State v. Kelly* (1984). The court relied on the work of psychologist, Lenore E. Walker to determine that the victim, who killed her husband in self-defense, suffered from "Battered Woman's Syndrome.[151] According to Walker, a victim who suffers from it is "one who is repeatedly subjected to any forceful or psychological behavior by a man in order to coerce her to do something he wants her to do without concern

148 *Id.* at 743.
149 *Id.* at 745.
150 SCHNEIDER ET AL., at 88.
151 *State v. Kelly* 97 N.J. 178; 478 A.2d 364, 371(1984).

for her rights."[152] The syndrome emphasizes the detrimental physical and mental challenges victims endure from being pressured by the abuser over time. Undergoing often constant, long-term harm and coercive control, "many [battered-women] strategically revise and cope with domestic violence."[153] Consequently, these victims have adopted certain survival mechanisms due to Post-Traumatic Stress Disorder (PTSD) that conceal their distress to the outside world and help them withstand their life behind closed doors.[154] In this sense, many victims have acquired coping mechanisms such as "learned helplessness" where they do not ultimately fight or flee their abuser.[155] Instead, they "freeze" and learn to make do with the harm.[156] Many battered women "become so demoralized and degraded by the fact that they cannot predict or control the violence that they sink into a state of psychological paralysis and become unable to take any action at all to improve or alter the situation."[157] Yet due to the complexity of the crime, the criminal justice system still does not fully acknowledge a victim's "learned helplessness" in order to help better understand the trauma of domestic abuse.

Domestic Violence and Popular Culture

Most of mainstream society continues to negate the seriousness of gender-based domestic violence especially when high-profile, public figures get away with it. Just as OJ Simpson famously eluded a domestic-murder conviction in 1994, certain sports figures help to minimize the public perception of domestic violence and reinforce sexist undertones when they receive little if any punishment. In 2014, Baltimore Raven's running back Ray Rice fought with his then-fiancée, Janay Palmer, beat her unconscious in an Atlantic City casino elevator, and dragged her body to the hotel room. The gruesome incident was captured by surveillance video, and it was the first time the public had witnessed the reality of such brutality. As a result, Rice was suspended from two National Football League (NFL) games and was indicted with third-degree aggravated assault.[158] Nonetheless, when the incident occurred, many members of the public did not agree with Rice's suspension: a poll conducted by Sports Illustrated Marketing and Research Resources indicated that only

152 *Id.* at 371.

153 Martha Chamallas, Introduction to Feminist Legal Theory, at 343 (Vol. 3 2013).

154 *Id.* at 341.

155 Dalton and Schneider, at 97.

156 Dalton and Schneider affirm that "battered women tend to 'give up' in the course of being abused; they suffer psychological paralysis" (107).

157 *State v. Kelly*, at 372.

158 Chris Wessling, *Ravens' Ray Rice Indicted for Aggravated Assault*, Around the NFL, (Mar. 30, 2014), http://www.nfl.com/news/story/0ap2000000337571/article/ravens-ray-rice-indicted-for-aggravated-assault.

28 percent of respondents felt that NFL players--including Rice--should be suspended when they are formally charged with a sexual or violent crime.[159] In fact, some members of the public not only responded with levity, but also with humor. For example, a "Ray Rice" Halloween costume became popular where men dressed in a Ravens uniform and carried a large doll by the hair on her head. So, although some agreed that Ray Rice deserved the criminal indictment, a good number dismissed the incident under the guise of frivolity.

Both Ray Rice and Janay Palmer also downplayed the life-threatening assault. Pleading not guilty to the aggravated assault charge that was eventually dropped, Rice publicly apologized for "the situation my wife and I were in."[160] By trivializing his actions, he faulted an external "situation,"—which implies it was something beyond his control. In addition, he also diminished his own accountability by blaming both himself and his wife. Unfortunately, Janay Palmer contributed to that assumption when she apologized for "her role that night."[161] As in the *Brown* case, Ms. Palmer implicitly faulted herself for his violent response, which helped to shift blame for Rice's actions. However, although there had been no reported histories of abuse between the pair, Ms. Palmer's answer could perhaps exist as part of the "learned helplessness" common to battered women.

After the incident, the Baltimore Ravens permanently released Ray Rice, and the NFL created a pre-emptive domestic violence program. Since then, however, Ray Rice has become the NFL's anti-domestic violence spokesperson, and this has been a topic of contention. Although Rice no longer plays for the NFL, he receives hefty compensation that has ultimately rewarded him for being a woman-beater. In other words, both the social and legal consequences of his actions have been minimal. However, indicating that the crime remains "hidden and often quite misunderstood," the NFL program works against domestic violence within the agency to prevent such crimes "before they happen."[162] The plan employs deterrent measures that include education classes, counseling, new rules for player conduct, and a minimum unpaid six-game suspension for those who commit domestic assault or sexual abuse.[163] Through the program, the NFL hopes to modify the "long-standing social norms" that permit domestic violence; however, the league recognizes that changing these cultural constructions will take time, effort, and resources.[164] Nonetheless, the creation of these new policies may serve as one step closer

159 NFL.com, *The NFL's Response to Domestic Violence and Sexual Assault*, NFL.com, (Dec. 5, 2014), https://www.nfl.com/news/the-nfl-s-response-to-domestic-violence-and-sexual-assault-0ap3000000439286

160 Wessling.

161 *Id.*

162 *NFL.com*

163 *Id.*

164 *Id.*

toward preventing these crimes and shifting the narrative within the professional sports community.

Conclusion

Black and Blue (1998) provides an illustration of how commonly held cultural assumptions about masculine authority in the domestic space encourages female submission, repression, and physical and psychological harm. While it was acceptable for a man to physically punish his wife during the colonial and Victorian time periods in America, both modern American society and the law still circuitously reinforce both conservative and extreme forms of violence. Although the Violence Against Women Act (VAMA) and other legislation has worked to improve protective measures for female victims, victims are still misunderstood, and the law remains limited. Due to intimacy and secrecy, domestic violence victims most often are left lost and alone. Many suffer from PTSD and remain frozen with indecision or lack of confidence. Just as *Black and Blue* depicts, the law offers very little, if any protection, and it tends to side with the abusers, instead. In the end, Beth Benedetto's husband, Bobby kidnaps their son, and she never sees him again. Despite the efforts of a private investigator, all leads to a dead end, and the audience is left with a sense of Beth's hopelessness and frustration of the system when she confirms, "What did the law ever do for me?"[165]

165 Quindlen, at 289.

4 Stalking

A Victim's Powerlessness Mistaken for Tolerance in *You* (2014)

Similar to sexual assault and domestic violence, history and statistics conclude that the crime of stalking has typically been motivated by sexist attitudes that devalue women.[1] Due to this fact, stalking disproportionately affects those who identify as female and can be considered a gendered form of violence.[2] Yet according to a recent study, although there are over three million stalking cases in the United States every year, only 7 percent of stalkers are arrested by the police and taken into custody.[3] Like sexual assault and domestic violence, the crime of stalking is also one that is rarely prosecuted. Part of the reason for this is because stalking is a crime like no other; a victim must prove a pattern of the stalking behavior through multiple incidents. This proves difficult since stalkers tend to be surreptitious. Most often there are no eyewitnesses, video surveillance, or DNA evidence. Thus, a causal link to the perpetrator does not exist. Like rapists, stalkers understand how to work the system, and they know that they can get away with the crime. As a result, many victims have been stalked for months, years, and even decades. In the rare event that a perpetrator is caught and prosecution takes place, it is often too late—the victim has most likely been seriously injured, kidnapped, or even murdered. So, despite the criminal and civil remedies, these measures typically offer no assistance to a victim of perpetual stalking. In this chapter, I argue that these victims suffer longstanding trauma from being stalked due to the lack of support or protection from law enforcement, the criminal justice system, and society at large.

1 Anna Miglietta and Daniela Acquadro Maran, *Gender, Sexism, and the Social Representation of Stalking: What Makes the Difference?* 7 Psychology of Violence 563, 563 (2017).

2 Kay Proctor, *Stalking as a Gender-Based Violence, in* The Routledge Handbook of Gender and Violence, 109, 113 (Nancy Lombard, ed. 2018).

3 *I Am a Stalker* (Netflix True Crime Documentaries, October 2022).

DOI: 10.4324/9781003303572-4

You (2014)

The novel *You* (2014) is written in first-person narrative by the narcissistic, habitual stalker, kidnapper, and murderer Joseph "Joe" Goldberg. The audience delves into the mindset of the bookstore clerk and his obsessive stages of stalking the graduate student and aspiring writer Guinevere "Beck" from the beginning, when he meets her, to the end, when he murders her. However, when he is first introduced to Beck, he begins to fixate on her, and she becomes an easy target for Joe to cyberstalk due to her unique name. By following her social media, he can track where she lives in New York City and where she meets her friends. Through this tracking system, he "accidentally" runs into her at a bar when she is drunk, and he uses the opportunity to steal her phone. After that point, he monitors her correspondences through email and learns more about her private life—her friendships, her habits, her likes and dislikes, and her relationships. In the beginning, he believes she will be an easy target due to her flirtatious, ditzy nature; however, he soon learns that she has attachment issues and emotional problems herself. As a result, she strings Joe along in a cycle of hot and cold behavior and interest and indifference. These actions only make him desire her more, and the audience witnesses the danger of his growing obsession with her. For example, to get some of Beck's "distractions" out of the way, he murders both an ex-boyfriend, Benji, for whom Beck has feelings, and a co-dependent friend, Peach, who secretly is in love with Beck. When Joe finally gets the romantic relationship he wants from Beck, she discovers many of her belongings that he stole in his apartment, and she accuses him of stalking her. Consequently, he kidnaps her and locks her in a cage that is designed for rare books in the store where he works. In the end, when she seduces him to gain his trust to escape, he murders her.

Stalking in the Media and in the Law

In the late 1980s, the public first became familiar with a real-life murder that derived from stalking when actress Rebecca Shaeffer was shot and killed by an obsessive fan, Robert John Bardo. Prior to the murder, Bardo had been stalking her for 2 years. In the end, he shot and killed her at the doorstep of her Los Angeles home. The case attracted extensive media coverage and elucidated the problematic nature of stalking. It also revealed that stalking was more common than the public realized, and it affected both celebrities and noncelebrities alike. However, at that time, anti-stalking laws were not in place, and police could not intervene even if the stalker repeatedly threatened the victim, sent her hate mail, or followed her.[4] In fact, "law enforcement could only take action after the suspect carried out his threats and assaulted

4 Donna Batten, *Stalking*, in Gale Encyclopedia of American Law, 322, 322 (3rd ed. 2010).

or injured the victim."[5] In this sense, the law then encouraged and even facilitated a stalker who wanted to physically harm a victim and get away with it. Frustrated and helpless, a victim sometimes endured years' worth of warning signs that ultimately escalated to assault, rape, robbery, or even murder. In the case of Rebecca Shaeffer, Bardo finally carried out his threats, and it resulted in her death. Consequently, in 1990, the state of California enacted the first anti-stalking law, and it became the model statute for other states. The current statute of the California Penal Code § 646.9 (2017) provides the following definition of stalking:

> (a) Any person who willfully, maliciously, and repeatedly follows or willfully and maliciously harasses another person and who makes a credible threat with the intent to place that person in reasonable fear for his or her safety, or the safety of his or her immediate family is guilty of the crime of stalking, punishable by imprisonment in a county jail for not more than one year, or by a fine of not more than one thousand dollars ($1,000), or by both that fine and imprisonment, or by imprisonment in the state prison.[6]

While most state legislation contains the same "basic core elements of stalking that include harassment and a credible threat," there are different requirements for the stalker's intent and a variety of penalties.[7] Yet to better understand the California law and most state statutes that follow, definitions of certain terms are relevant to the interpretation of the legislation. For example, "harassment" means that the stalker knowingly and willingly "seriously alarms, annoys, torments, or terrorizes" the victim without a legitimate purpose.[8] "Course of conduct" occurs when the stalker exhibits a pattern of behavior over a period of time.[9] A "credible threat" may be express or implied, and the prosecution does not have to prove that the stalker intended to harm the victim or carry out the threat.[10] Instead, a prosecutor must prove that the defendant "intended to place the victim in fear."[11]

5 *Id.* at 322.

6 CAL. PENAL CODE § 646.9 (2017).

7 KERRY WELLS, *Prosecuting Those Who Stalk: A Prosecutor's Legal Perspective and Viewpoint*, in STALKING CRIMES AND VICTIM PROTECTION: PREVENTION INTERVENTION, THREAT ASSESSMENT, AND CASE MANAGEMENT, 427, 428 (Joseph A. Davis, ed., 2001).

8 WELLS, at 428. See also *People v. Heilman* 25 Cal. App. 4th 391 (1994), which defines "harassment" as "multiple acts" and "course of conduct" as "a series of acts, over a period of time, *however short*, evidencing continuity of purpose."

9 WELLS, at 429. In *People v. McCray* (1997), the California appellate court held that the pattern of behavior over time may be in as little as one day. 58 Cal. App. 4th 159.

10 WELLS, at 431.

11 *Id.* at 431.

Legal Civil Remedy: Restraining Order

Before a stalker is arrested, a victim's first legal remedy includes obtaining a protective restraining order in a civil court.[12] Under the order, a stalker cannot be in the vicinity of the victim. If a stalker violates the order, he may be punished by being held in contempt of court, by paying a fine, or by being incarcerated, depending on the state's law.[13] Nonetheless, these orders often prove ineffective because they are difficult to enforce, and stalkers tend to escape punishment when they violate the order. Nonetheless, if a stalker violates a protective order, many states increase a sentence from a misdemeanor to a felony, and punishment can range from 3 to 5 years in jail.[14] By contrast, without the violation of a protective order, many states include a misdemeanor charge of stalking that is punishable by a jail sentence of up to one year.[15]

Anti-Stalking Laws and Constitutional Challenges

Federal statutes have also been enacted to protect victims of stalking. For instance, the Violence Against Women Act (VAWA) authorizes a nationwide enforcement of protective orders.[16] In addition, the Interstate Stalking Act makes it a criminal offense to travel from one state to another to stalk another person.[17] This includes stalking a person across state lines via email or via the internet, and such crimes are punishable from 5 years to life in prison.[18] Yet due to the ease of anonymity on the internet, online bullies, criminals, and harassers are rarely prosecuted because police do not have the necessary training to track them down. Thus, legal remedies in civil court and state and federal statutes tend to fail the victim in most circumstances. As a result, many victims do not report the crime due to privacy issues, and most know that police efforts will prove unsuccessful.[19] In fact, the only time stalking—internet or otherwise—tends to be successfully prosecuted is if a companion or crossover crime such as kidnapping, assault, burglary, or murder also occurs.[20] Due to such rare instances of prosecution, some critics argue that the court system

12 Batten, at 323.
13 *Id.*
14 Batten, at 323.
15 Batten, at 323: Enhanced penalties that increase a sentence from a misdemeanor to a felony include "if the defendant brandished a gun, violated a protective order, committed a previous stalking offense, or directed his conduct toward a child."
16 18 U.S.C.A. § 2265–2266 [2000]
17 18 U.S.C.A. § 2261A [1996]
18 18 U.S.C.A § 2261A [1996]
19 Batten, at 323.
20 Neal Miller, *Stalking Investigation, Law, Public Policy, and Criminal Prosecution as Problem Solver*, in Stalking Crimes and Victim Protection: Prevention, Intervention, Threat Assessment, and Case Management, 387, 397. (Joseph A. Davis, ed. 2001).

proves too lenient in sentencing stalkers. Other commentators contend that neither prosecutors nor police take the crime seriously and ultimately do not adequately protect victims.[21] Consequently, many argue that both state and federal laws against stalking are only symbolic ones with little operative and practical effect.

In the rare event that a stalker has been successfully prosecuted, sometimes the accused challenges the constitutionality of the state statute. For example, some assert that the statute is too vague under the Due Process Clause.[22] On the contrary, others claim that the legislation is too broad and infringes upon constitutionally protected speech. One example is found in *People v. Ashley* (2020), where the Supreme Court of Illinois upheld the state anti-stalking statute against both Due Process and First Amendment violation claims.[23] In this case, the defendant had been convicted of felony stalking. The Supreme Court of Illinois determined that the defendant's verbal and text-message threats to kill the victim and her mother were not protected speech under the First Amendment.[24] The court further held that the state statute did not violate due process by prohibiting "speech that 'threatens'."[25] Similar to this decision, the majority of courts have rejected these types of constitutionality challenges and upheld the anti-stalking laws.

Stalking Behaviors

Like sexual assault and domestic violence convictions, penalties from the criminal court are rare because the elements of stalking are particularly difficult to prove "beyond a reasonable doubt." However, one solution could be to focus on the stalker's behavior instead of his intent to "knowingly or willingly" harass a victim because stalking behaviors tend to be overt and easier to prove.[26] For instance, some examples of stalking behaviors include, but are not limited to, "going through mail or stealing it, entering the home to move around objects without taking anything, using other persons to help in the stalking, stealing underwear, going through the victim's garbage, threatening suicide ... ordering or canceling things in the victim's name (such as utilities,

21 Batten, at 324.

22 Some additional examples where vagueness has been rejected are *State v. Randall*, 669 So2d 223 [Ala Ct Crim App 1995]; *Peterson v. State*, 930 P2d 414 [Alaska Ct App 1996]; *People v. Ewing*, 76 Cal App 4th 199 [Cal Ct App 1999] [and cases cited at 206, n2]; *People v. Baer*, 973 P2d 1225 [Colo 1999]; *State v. Marsala*, 688 A2d 336 [Conn Ct App], cert denied 690 A2d 400 [Conn 1997]; *United States v. Smith*, 685 A2d 380 [DC 1997]; *Snowden v. State*, 677 A2d 33 [Del 1996]

23 People v. Ashley, 16, 1–18, 2020 IL 123989 (Sup. Ct. IL 2020).

24 *Id.* at 17.

25 *Id.* at 18.

26 U.S. Dept. of Justice, Bureau of Justice Assistance, *Regional Seminar Series on Developing and Implementing Anti-Stalking Codes*, NCJ-156836 (June 1996).

leases, subscriptions, etc.), or harassing the victim's neighbors, friends, family, or children."[27] Oftentimes the behavior is so strange that a victim has difficulty convincing others that it even happened. For example, some stalking victims have reported unusual behavior such as finding their clothes cut into pieces or discovering semen on the steering wheel of their car.[28] Since stalkers can become quite creative in their harassment, the experience can be frustrating, frightening, and alienating. Even more so, victims who have been stalked for months or even years at a time may suffer ongoing trauma akin to "psychological terrorism."[29]

Typologies of Stalking

To understand the psychology of stalkers, researchers, practitioners, and law enforcement have created three different typologies of stalking in cis-gender male perpetrator/female victim pairings.[30] The common theme in these typologies includes the stalker's obsession with the victim; nonetheless, the psychological motivations may vary. For example, in the "simple obsessional" typology, the stalker and victim have had a prior relationship; however, he attempts to "lure the victim back into a relationship, [due to] anger or loss of control or feelings of mistreatment, and [a desire for] revenge."[31] By contrast, the victim and stalker have not had a relationship in the "love obsessional" typology, but the stalker considers the victim an object of love and adoration.[32] In these instances, some stalkers may suffer psychiatric disorders such as schizophrenia or borderline personality disorder, while others may be "socially maladjusted."[33] In this particular category, perpetrators also often stalk public figures.[34] Conversely, in the last classification—"erotomaniac"—the defining characteristic includes a stalker who believes the victim is in love with him.[35] In these cases, sometimes the stalker may blame others, such as the victim's spouse or boyfriend, for the victim's failure to acknowledge or return the stalker's affections.[36] Yet whether the stalker belongs in an "erotomaniac,"

27 Doris M. Hall, *Victims of Stalking*, in THE PSYCHOLOGY OF STALKING: CLINICAL AND FORENSIC PERSPECTIVES, 113, 132. (J. Reid Meloy, ed. 1998).

28 *Id.* at 132–133.

29 *Id.* at 133.

30 Miller, at 398. See also, Glen Skoler, *The Archetypes and Psychodynamics of Stalking*, in THE PSYCHOLOGY OF STALKING: CLINICAL AND FORENSIC PERSPECTIVES, 96, 85. (John Reid Meloy, ed. 1998); John Reid Meloy, *Stalking. An Old Behavior, a New Crime*, in 22.1 March THE PSYCHIATRIC CLINICS OF NORTH AMERICA 89, 85 (1999).

31 Miller, at 398.

32 *Id.*

33 *Id.*

34 *Id.*

35 *Id.*

36 *Id.*

a "love obsessional," or a "simple obsessional" category, all stalkers possess an unhealthy fixation or preoccupation with the victim.

Stalking and Gendered-Based Violence

Regardless of the psychological motivations, in male stalker–female victim scenarios, sexism is typically a prevailing characteristic, and researchers have concluded that stalking is a form of gender-based violence.[37] As victim's rights attorney and stalking specialist Carrie Goldberg puts it, "intimate partner stalking often exists as part of a constellation of misogynist and violent behavior."[38] Many scholars have determined that social conditioning and sexist attitudes toward females provide rationale as to why men typically stalk women in cis-gender heterosexual pairings.[39] Stalking, then, as a form of gender-based violence, is a product of a longstanding form of gender inequality.[40] Many male stalkers rationalize their behavior with outdated, traditional social norms that reinforce male superiority over women. Historically, these values have perpetuated physical violence between the genders. For example, while both men and women may become aggressive in their relationships, a woman's violence against a man typically does not threaten his sense of safety and wellbeing.[41] On the other hand, a male abuser most often instills fear and a mechanism to control the female victim.[42]

Other gendered patterns in stalking differentiate between the male and female experience. Specifically, women tend to feel more frightened and threatened by their stalkers, while male victims of female stalkers typically

37 Katy Proctor, *Stalking as a Gender-Based Violence*, in The Routledge Handbook of Gender and Violence 109, 117 (Nancy Lombard, ed., 2018)

38 Carrie Goldberg, Nobody's Victim: Fighting Psychos, Stalkers, Pervs, and Trolls 20 (2019).

39 H. Colleen Sinclair, *Stalking Myth Attributions: Examining the Role of Individual and Contextual Variables on Unwanted Pursuit Scenarios*, in Sex Roles 378, 379 (2012).; Alice H. Eagly, Anne E. Beall, & Robert J. Sternberg, eds., The Psychology of Gender, 4 (2005); Lorraine Sheridan, Raphael Gillett, and Graham Davies, *Stalking: Seeking the Victim's Perspective*, in 6 Psychology, Crime, & Law, 267, 267 (2012).

40 R. Emerson Dobash and Russell Dobash, Violence Against Wives (1979); Elizabeth Stanko, *Theorizing About Violence Observations From the Economic and Social Research Council's Violence Research Program*, in Violence Against Women 543, 543 (2006); Evan Stark, Coercive Control: How Men Entrap Women in Personal Life (2007).

41 Russell Dobash and R. Emerson Dobash, *Women's Violence to Men in Intimate Relationships: Working on a Puzzle*, 44.3 The British Journal of Criminology 324, 324 (2004).

42 Michael P. Johnson, *Patriarchal Terrorism and Common Couple Violence: Two Forms of Violence Against Women*, 57.2 Journal of Marriage and the Family 283, 283 (1995); Michael P. Johnson, *Conflict Control: Gender Symmetry and Asymmetry in Domestic Violence*, 12.11 Violence Against Women 1003, 1003 (2006); Marianne Hester, Who Does What to Whom? Gender and Domestic Violence Perpetrators (2009).

do not report feelings of fear or intimidation.[43] In fact, whereas female victims who are perpetually stalked often resort to changing their social behaviors, modifying their interpersonal relationships, or moving from their home to a different location, male victims are "less likely to give up activities and less likely to feel distrustful of others."[44] On the other hand, not only do most female victims feel threatened, but they also believe their stalker will carry out those threats.[45] In fact, there is a greater risk of a male stalker fulfilling his threats with "approaching behaviors," and women are more likely to report being physically harmed, to seek counsel, and to call the police.[46] All these gendered patterns suggest that male perpetrators tend to be more aggressive and persistent in stalking behaviors and female victims to feel a greater impact from being stalked.

The Anatomy of a Stalker: Joe Goldberg in *You*

In the novel *You* (2014), Joe Goldberg stalks his victim, Guinevere Beck, before, during, and after their relationship ends. As scholar John Reid Meloy puts it, "stalking is a chronic behavior that unfolds over the course of months or even years."[47] After their initial meeting at the bookstore where he works, Joe immediately begins fantasizing about Beck, comparing her to the character played by Natalie Portman in the movie *Closer* when "she's fresh-faced and done with bad British guys."[48] Dressed in pink, Beck is pretty, friendly, and feminine. Joe becomes smitten by her appearance and by what he believes as her passivity and politeness. She stops to say hello to Joe "when other people would just pass by."[49] When she goes out of her way to be courteous to him, he automatically becomes infatuated. In this sense, Joe's immediate and intense fixation provides an example of how some stalkers contrive narcissistic fantasies that "often form the basis of romantic pursuit, instilled with hope and idealization of the future."[50] He goes so far as to believe that Beck is a special gift from the universe, and he marvels that she has "come home to [him], delivered at last."[51]

43 Beth Bjerregaard, *An Empirical Study of Stalking Victimisation,* 15.4 VIOLENCE AND VICTIMS 389, 389 (2000).

44 PAUL E. MULLEN, ET AL. STALKERS AND THEIR VICTIMS (2nd ed. 2009).

45 Bjerregaard, at 389.

46 *Id.*

47 John Reid Meloy, *Stalking. An Old Behavior, a New Crime*, in 22.1 March THE PSYCHIATRIC CLINICS OF NORTH AMERICA 85, 89 (1999).

48 KEPNES, at 1.

49 *Id.*

50 Meloy, *Stalking. An Old Behavior, a New Crime*, at 88.

51 KEPNES, at 1.

After their initial meeting, Joe stealthily pursues Beck to learn more about her and to establish a disingenuous connection based on manipulation and a false sense of familiarity. He does this through online spying, scheming, lies, and covert abuse that violates her privacy. This stalking scenario provides an example of a "pernicious and largely unacknowledged form of partner abuse," that "[is] within the context of intimate relationships."[52] Joe disregards mutual, truthful interest, respect, and trust between two people in a romantic relationship. Instead, he relies on a dishonest attempt to control Beck through her vulnerabilities. In this sense, initially Joe begins as a "love obsessional" stalker. However, after he wins her over, the "love obsessional" stalker becomes a "simple obsessional" stalker since the two then engage in an on-again, off-again relationship.

Upon Joe's instantaneous obsession with Beck, he immerses himself in her life and quickly forgets about his own interests. Joe's behavior coincides with scholars Melita Schaum's and Karen Parrish's explanation about how in the "early stages of stalking, the boundaries between normal persistence and obsessive behaviors" become blurred.[53] For instance, after saving the credit card receipt from the bookstore with her full name on it, Joe creates a well-planned and elaborate stalking regime. He begins to spy on her at her home and even goes so far as to disguise himself by wearing various outfits every night so neither she nor her neighbors will recognize him.[54] He becomes consumed with Beck's life and his attempts to impress her. Joe spends all his free time studying her, and he weaves together a web of intricate, pernicious practices. For example, after three months of spying on her, he schemes to get into her apartment by reporting a gas leak and claiming to be her boyfriend. In addition, after he discovers that Beck casually dates a man named Benji, he resolves to remove her "distraction." He accomplishes this task by impersonating a food critic to meet Benji, who owns a club soda company. Then he drugs and kidnaps Benji, hacks into his social media and email accounts, "breaks up" with Beck, and then murders him.[55]

Although stalkers who commit homicide are rare, Joe nonetheless provides the example of a stalker who "is a product of a narcissistic pathology."[56] According to the DSM-III, narcissistic personality disorder is defined as "a pervasive pattern of grandiosity (fantasy or behavior), need for admiration, and a lack of empathy, beginning at early adulthood" to the point of

52 Goldberg, at 17.

53 Melita Schaum and Karen Parish, Stalked: Breaking the Silence on the Crime of Stalking in America, 105 (1995).

54 Kepnes, at 15.

55 *Id.* at 70.

56 Bran Nicol, Stalking, 7 (2006).

"significant distress or dysfunction."[57] A person diagnosed with this disorder must possess at least five of the nine criteria:

1. Possesses a grandiose sense of self-importance (e.g., exaggerates achievements, expects to be recognized as superior without actually completing the achievements).
2. Is preoccupied with fantasies of success, power, brilliance, beauty, or perfect love.
3. Believes that they are special and unique and can only be understood by or should only associate with other special people (or institutions).
4. Requires excessive admiration.
5. Has a sense of entitlement, such as an unreasonable expectation of favorable treatment or compliance with his or her expectations.
6. Engages in interpersonal exploitation and takes advantage of others to achieve their own ends.
7. Lacks empathy; is unwilling to identify with the needs of others.
8. Is often envious of others or believes that others are envious of them.
9. Shows arrogant, haughty behaviors and attitudes.[58]

Although not all stalkers are diagnosed with narcissistic personality disorder, some studies have concluded that the disorder may be found in up to 60 percent of stalkers.[59] Narcissistic stalkers are particularly dangerous because they "form intense, [abnormal], preoccupied attachments to their victims."[60]

Stalking and the Internet

Another way in which stalkers may perpetuate their fixation on victims is through the internet. For example, in *You,* Joe easily discovers the unique name "Guinevere Beck" online. He quickly finds her social media accounts

57 American Psychiatric Association, Diagnostic and Statistical Manual of Mental Disorders, 669 (5th ed. 2013). See also Alan C. Logan and Susan L. Prescott, *Plenary Health: We Need to Talk About Narcissism,* Challenges 1, 3 (2022).

58 American Psychiatric Association, Diagnostic and Statistical Manual of Mental Disorders, 669 (5th ed. 2013).

59 R.D. Hare, *Manual for the Psychopathy Checklist-Revised,* MultiHealth Systems (1991). See also: John Reid Meloy, *Stalking (Obsessional Following): A Review of Some Preliminary Studies* 1 Aggression and Violent Behavior 147, 147 (1996).

60 Meloy, *Stalking. An Old Behavior, A New Crime* at 87. See also Glen Lipson and Mark Mills, *Erotomania and the Tarasoff Cases,* in The Psychology of Stalking: Clinical and Forensic Perspectives 257, 257 (John Reid Meloy, ed. 1998); John Reid Meloy, *Unrequited Love and the Wish to Kill: Diagnosis and Treatment of Borderline Erotomania,* 53 Bull Menninger Clinic 477, 477 (1989); John Reid Meloy, *Stalking (Obsessional Following): A Review of Some Preliminary Studies,* 1 Aggression and Violent Behavior 147, 147 (1996).

and learns about her through Twitter and her blog posts about being a writer and an MFA graduate student at New York University.[61] When Beck tags her location in her posts, Joe can track her down to the bars, restaurants, and other places she frequents. He begins to understand her habits and interests through the information she divulges online. He explains that from his perspective, "the internet is a beautiful thing" because she is easy to "flesh out" due to her "revealing bios."[62] By stalking her online, he also learns about her family, her upbringing, and where she has lived.[63] The ease by which Joe discovers details of Beck's personal life demonstrates that the internet is dangerous for victims and delightful for stalkers. Many people who post information online do not realize they can become targets of perpetrators with bad intentions, and private information may be found with little effort. In fact, in a 2009 legislative report, law enforcement estimated that "electronic communications are a factor in 20–40 percent of stalking cases."[64] However, because technology has become even more advanced since 2009 and because cyberstalking, trolling, and online bullying have become more prevalent since then, we can assume that the percentage of these cases has exponentially increased.[65]

Joe's Stalking Pattern of Behavior

As Joe uses the internet to invade Beck's private life, he creates a false sense of security between the two, and because of his ruse, they begin to become closer and spend more time together. However, the audience does not realize the extent of Joe's obsession until Beck surprises him at his apartment one day, and he quickly becomes anxious that she will discover many of her stolen belongings. At that point, the audience learns that he has broken into her home multiple times and has taken her clothing, underwear, a bottle of iced tea, and a hair clip with a few of her hair strands on it—things that "hold [her] DNA, [and her] scent."[66] By collecting these items, Joe feels closer to Beck, and since he views her as a possession, he feels entitled to come into her home and take her personal effects without permission. However, when faced with a realistic fear of getting caught, he is suddenly struck with the consequences

61 Kepnes, at 11.

62 *Id.* at 12–13.

63 *Id.* at 11–13.

64 National Conference of State Legislators, *Cyberbullying and the States* (2009).

65 Jonathan Bishop states that "police and criminal justice agencies report difficulties in keeping up with the rise in number of reports of online crime and abuse, while there are currently ineffective means of legislating against and/or investigating and prosecuting cases." *The Art of Trolling Law Enforcement: A Review and Model for Implementing "Flame Trolling" Legislation Enacted in Great Britain (1981–2012) in* 27.3 International Review of Law, Computers, and Technology 301, 301 (2013).

66 Kepnes, at 221.

of his actions that could result in him losing her. In other words, he does not feel remorse for his actual behavior. Instead, he feels fear of being found out and being punished for his misdeeds.

However, to his relief, Joe does not get caught during Beck's surprise visit, so as a result, their relationship progresses, and he finally gets his wish of having sex with her. Nonetheless, his happiness is short-lived because a few days later, Beck stands him up on their next date. Reacting to the disappointment, he severely punishes himself for it. He uncovers his self-hatred by calling himself "a limp dick pussy."[67] He also engages in self-harm by severely burning his finger with a candle flame.[68] Like the surprising incident where Joe disclosed his collection of Beck's possessions, this scene reveals his extreme self-contempt for the first time. Although up until then, his attitude was one of arrogance, entitlement, and self-righteousness, the audience begins to see his desperate fragility and insecurity. After having sex, Joe believed he was finally in control of his object of affection. Nevertheless, his excessive feelings of abandonment were triggered after Beck withdrew her attention. For the narcissistic stalker, "rejection stimulates shame and humiliation."[69] Therefore, the only way Joe copes with the intensity of disappointment is by turning his rage on himself. To that end, John Reid Meloy confirms that rage after rejection is a typical pattern for most stalkers.[70] Moreover, the stalker then uses that anger as fuel and as further motivation to hurt, control, damage, or destroy the victim.[71] Under "normal" circumstances, rejection might cause someone to let go and move on; however, the narcissistic stalker becomes even more fixated on the victim. Consequently, the emotional pain from rejection results in an even deeper attachment to the victim and to his fantasy.[72]

As the novel progresses, the audience witnesses firsthand Joe's elevated obsession with Beck. What results includes an escalation of his stalking behaviors that leads not only to more violence but ultimately to murder.[73] Joe's mood, happiness, and mental stability completely depend on Beck's real or perceived attention. When he hacks into her email and sees Beck wrote to a friend that "she misses him," he feels overcome with complete elation and irrational desire.[74] Although she has not spoken to him for over two weeks, he jumps to conclusions and acts on the fantasy that she wants to see him. This

67 Kepnes, at 248.

68 *Id.*

69 Meloy, *Stalking. A New Behavior, an Old Crime,* 88.

70 *Id.*

71 *Id.*

72 *Id.*

73 *I Am a Stalker* (Netflix True Crime Documentaries, October 2022). When the duration, frequency, and intensity (DIF) of stalking begin to escalate even further, the probability of continued violence increases as well.

74 Kepnes, at 256.

behavior embodies the DSM-III criterion for narcissistic personality disorder in that Joe possesses an "unreasonable expectation of favorable treatment or compliance with his expectations."[75] This erroneous belief based on fantasy creates an overwhelming desire to track Beck down, even after he is beaten badly during a burglary at the bookstore. Bleeding, bruised, and driving in bad road conditions with an unreliable car, his one motivation is to orchestrate a chance encounter to see her in Little Compton, where he discovers she is staying with a wealthy friend from college, Peach Salinger.[76] His entire happiness and wellbeing depend on seeing her, and he places his own physical safety in grave danger. Although he has an accident and gets knocked unconscious after hitting a deer in the road, when he wakes up, the only thing on his mind is waiting for Beck's text message or call so they can meet.

Target Dispersion

His stalking behaviors and heightened motivation to see Beck continue to escalate when Joe breaks into Peach's mansion while the women are out. He audaciously makes himself coffee and takes some of Beck's clothes—including her underwear. Later, when they return, he spies on the two women and witnesses Beck and Peach getting into a fight after Beck refuses Peach's sexual advances. The next day when Peach goes out alone for a run, he follows her, strangles her, loads her pockets with rocks, and dumps her in the ocean. With her phone, he writes Beck an email from "Peach" that implies she committed suicide.[77] Similar to Benji's kidnapping and murder, Joe engages in a stalking practice called "target dispersion."[78] This occurs when a stalker begins to spy on people who are close to the primary victim such as friends, romantic partners, and family. In extreme cases such as with Peach and Benji, Joe not only spies on them but also murders them. Under these circumstances, Joe considers both friends of Beck as not only a distraction but also a threat. Viewing her as a possession, he becomes more and more frustrated when Beck chooses to spend time with others aside from him. As a result, he increases the intensity of his stalking from spying and anonymous harassment to physical violence.

75 American Psychiatric Association, Diagnostic and Statistical Manual of Mental Disorders, at 669.

76 Kepnes, at 262.

77 *Id.* at 288.

78 John Reid Meloy, Molly Amman, and Jens Hoffman, *9 Public Figure Stalking and Attacks, in* International Handbook of Threat Assessment, 166, 166 (John Reid Meloy, Molly Amman, and Jens Hoffman, eds., 2nd ed 2021).

DARVO and Justification for Beck's Murder

In the end, Joe's increased acts of violence ultimately result in his murdering Beck. Although Joe and Beck initially become intimate on a more regular basis after the incident in Little Compton, the relationship only lasts a few weeks. When Beck once again pulls away, Joe becomes even more desperate by stalking and plotting to murder her therapist, Dr. Nicky. Yet before he can carry out his plan, Beck finally finds out about Joe one day when she arrives at his apartment while he is away. She lets herself in, goes through his things, and finds his "Box of Beck" which includes a used tampon, her glasses, her yearbook, and other intimate belongings.[79] However, when Joe gets there and she confronts him by calling him a "sicko," he downplays his behavior.[80] He immediately gaslights her and shifts the blame when he tells her "you're the one who snooped in *my* wall yet you're acting like I'm the only one with problems."[81] With this singular comment, Joe reverses any accountability of all his stalking and violence and even justifies these actions when he denies, attacks, then reverses the victim and offender (DARVO).[82] Although researchers have found that perpetrators of domestic and sexual violence commonly employ DARVO, it is also a behavior that "has been used by generations of stalkers … to avoid detection and evade confrontation."[83] In this case, Joe uses DARVO as an excuse to kidnap Beck, imprison her in the cage at the bookstore, and ultimately murder her. Even as he strangles the life out of her, he blames her for his violence when he calls her "a monster, deathly, solipsistic to the bone."[84]

Sexist Stereotypes and Justification of Stalking

Yet from the beginning, Joe rationalizes his stalking and violence not only through DARVO but also through sexism and his hypermasculine ideals.[85] Like Bobby Benedetto in *Black and Blue,* Joe believes in traditional gender roles that reinforce masculine power and authority over females. To hypermasculine men, females are most often viewed as inferior simply due to their

79 Kepnes, at 370–371.

80 *Id.* at 370.

81 *Id.* See also Carrie Goldberg, Nobody's Victim, at 21: "These guys are master manipulators, skilled at gaslighting and distorting the truth."

82 Jennifer J. Freyd, *Violations of Power, Adaptive Blindness, and Betrayal Trauma Theory* in Feminism and Psychology, 22, 22 (1997).

83 Darvo, A Stalker's Strategy for Avoiding Exposure, Toxic Lives (Nov. 2017), https://strugl.org/darvo-a-stalkers-strategy-for-avoiding-exposure-8th-august-2017/

84 Kepnes, at 410.

85 See How Narcissists Use DARVO to Escape Accountability, NAR (Narcissistic Abuse Rehab) (Apr. 30, 2020), https://www.narcissisticabuserehab.com/darvo/

gender. On the contrary, men are considered stronger, smarter, wiser, and more capable because they are men. These hypermasculine concepts metamorphose into characteristics of toxic masculinity when these stereotypes are used as justification for harming women. Specifically in the case of Bobby and Joe, both men believe they can abuse their female victims because they are entitled to do so.

By focusing solely on Beck's attractive physical attributes, Joe otherwise sees her as superficial, unintelligent, and weak. Viewing her as only a sex object, he describes her as "full of disclaimers ... like a warning label on a pack of cigarettes."[86] Yet Joe also openly admits to and owns his sexism. For example, after Joe finally wins Beck over, he hires her to work with him in the bookstore. He ruminates, "we are like one of those 1950's couples, very sexist, because I am in charge, and you like it that way."[87] However, one day he becomes annoyed by what she wears to work. To Joe, the slouchy sweater that falls off one shoulder to reveal Beck's collarbone is "a boner-inducing porno shot."[88] Although Beck dutifully decides to go home and change when Joe criticizes her clothing, she takes it as a flirtatious compliment instead of a sexist insult. Part of the reason why Joe is attracted to Beck is because she possesses many hyperfeminine characteristics that suggest she is both passive and submissive to men, and Joe is drawn to what he perceives as her feminine weakness, which compliments his perception of male superiority.

Joe assumes Beck's femininity is a weakness due to what he perceives as her hyperfeminine traits. Hyperfemininity is defined as "an exaggerated adherence to ... stereotypic feminine gender roles."[89] Hyperfeminine women tend to place their value and worth on their sexuality and believe their success is rooted in acquiring and maintaining a relationship with a man.[90] Certain characteristics these women possess include an emphasis on their physical appearance and sexuality, passivity, and agreeability toward men. In general, they tend to portray an accommodating, obedient attitude toward male authority. Due to these features, they attract hypermasculine men who, like hyperfeminine women, typically conform to conventional gender norms. These hypermasculine men embody a "callous [and often demeaning] attitude toward women," and connect the notion of "manliness" to violence and danger.[91] Thus, aggressive, dominant hypermasculine men often appeal to acquiescent hyperfeminine female partners and vice versa.

86 Kepnes, at 12.
87 *Id.* at 237.
88 *Id.* at 238.
89 Sarah K. Murnen and Donn Byrne. *Hyperfemininity: Measurement and Initial Validation of the Construct* in 28.3 Journal of Sex Research, 479, 480 (1991).
90 Murnen and Byrne, at 480.
91 Donald L. Mosher and Mark Sirkin. *Measuring a Macho Personality Consternation* in 18.2 Journal of Research Personality, 150, 150 (1984).

Hyperfemininity and Victimology in *You*

A dangerous, violent hypermasculine stalker like Joe consciously or unconsciously views a hyperfeminine woman like Beck as an easy target and someone he can control. When he first sees her at the bookstore, Beck embodies all the characteristics to which he is attracted. She is dressed in pink—a color typically categorized as "feminine." She also exemplifies the stereotypical ideal of female beauty: pretty, blonde, and petite. In addition to her appearance, she possesses a cheerful, polite disposition. To certain men, this suggests she prioritizes others' views, ideas, and comfort over her own.[92] So Joe becomes especially intrigued when he observes that she goes out of her way to be nice.[93]

However, as the novel progresses, the audience learns that Beck uses her good looks and hyperfemininity to conceal her true feelings of insecurity and her low self-esteem. Although Beck is young, attractive, and intelligent, she is constantly distracted by portraying a "perfect," disingenuous life on social media. She also sets herself up for failure by attempting to continually impress her wealthy, superficial friends when she comes from a working-class background with limited financial means. Lacking self-confidence, she seeks approval outside of herself—not only from friends and from the internet, but also from men. Her fragile ego and lack of self-respect attract her to men who usually only see her as a sex object.[94] She also flirts with many men at once and falls for those who are ultimately emotionally unavailable—like Benji, a "sociopathic party boy;" Dr. Nicky, her middle-aged, married therapist; and Joe, the narcissistic stalker and murderer.[95] Thus, Beck chooses emotionally detached, neglectful, damaged, and sometimes even cruel men.

Like Francine Benedetto in *Black and Blue*, Beck also comes from an unstable family life and a broken home, which most likely contributes to her insecurity and lack of self-confidence. After Joe meets Beck and begins stalking her, he hacks into Beck's online account and discovers she has what he refers to as "daddy issues."[96] He learns that her parents are divorced, and her father remarried a wealthy woman. Beck's relationship with her father is strained, and they do not see each other often. On the rare occasion when they spend time together, Beck's father treats her poorly, and they fight most of the

92 According to Brijana Prooker, "women's pathological politeness" is "an everlasting ploy of the patriarchy." Women and girls have been socialized to be courteous, "often at the expense of their safety and well-being." *It's Time for Women to Break Up With Politeness,* Elle (Apr. 14, 2021) https://www.elle.com/culture/a35854625/no-more-politeness-2021/

93 KEPNES, at 1.

94 According to Joana Pantazi, low self-worth is the reason why certain people seek out and stay in toxic relationships. *10 Reasons Why We Stay in Toxic Relationships,* YOUNIVERSE (Sept. 19, 2019) https://www.youniversetherapy.com/post/10-reasons-why-we-stay-in-toxic-relationships

95 KEPNES, at 30.

96 *Id.* at 68.

time. Overall, the relationship lacks trust, open and honest communication, and respect. Most likely as a result, Beck avoids true intimacy and genuine connections with men. To that end, Joe discovers that she likes to "reel in men" and then loses interest when she has them, and she enjoys being objectified and admits to not wearing a bra in order to get attention.[97] Ultimately, Beck chases after men who do not want her, and Joe finds this emotional instability attractive.[98] To him, her propensity to self-sabotage appears as a weakness to which he can control, and in the end, Joe uses it against Beck not only to continue to manipulate and stalk her but also to kidnap and murder her.

Stalking Trauma Syndrome, Learned Helplessness, and the Freeze Response

While there are no scholarly sources that specifically correlate a victim's freeze response to being stalked, studies show that victims of long-time stalking suffer from a specific form of Post Traumatic Stress Disorder (PTSD) called Stalking Trauma Syndrome (STS).[99] This syndrome is closely linked to Battered Woman's Syndrome and the trauma experienced by victims of domestic violence. However, STS differs from Battered Woman's Syndrome due to the unique type of stress from which stalking victims typically suffer. Namely, while the cycle of "domestic violence consists of three phases: tension building, active battering, and making up in the 'honeymoon phase,'" STS replaces the cycle of domestic violence with a "cycle of crisis."[100] This cycle of crisis consists of "three phases: the crisis phase, the recovery phase, and the anticipation phase."[101] While there is no acute "active battering" or violence that begins and ends as in the domestic violence cycle, a stalking victim suffers repeated psychological trauma during the crisis phase.[102] With a repetition of offenses such as harassment, intimidation, threats, or violence, "the type of victimization present in stalking does not appear to have a definite beginning or a definite end."[103] As stalking tends to intensify over time, the recovery phase becomes brief or nonexistent, and the victim "only experiences the crisis phase and the anticipation phase again and again."[104] As a result, the

97 *Id.* at 292.

98 *Id.*

99 Melissa J. Collins and Mary Beth Wilkas, *Stalking Tramua Syndrome and the Traumatized Victim*, in STALKING CRIMES AND VICTIM PROTECTION: PREVENTION, INTERVENTION, THREAT ASSESSMENT, AND CASE MANAGEMENT 317, 319 (Joseph A. Davis, ed., 2001).

100 Collins and Wilkas, at 320.

101 *Id.*

102 *Id.*

103 *Id.* at 321.

104 *Id.* at 323.

victim becomes consumed with constant alarm, dread, and hypervigilance.[105] In other words, the victim lives in a persistent state of fear without reprieve.[106]

By remaining in a state of fright, a stalking victim may develop a form of learned helplessness that is different from that of domestic violence victims.[107] For example, in STS, the victim does not have a constant, ongoing relationship with her abuser and does not have the choice of changing her behavior to stop the abuse.[108] She also does not have the option of leaving the abusive situation since she is subjected to an uncontrollable environment from which she cannot escape.[109] However, like domestic violence victims, many stalking victims acquire coping mechanisms such as "learned helplessness" where, in the end, they cannot or do not ultimately fight or flee from their abuser. While victims may initially try to fight their stalker by reporting the crime, most do not receive adequate assistance from law enforcement or support from the criminal justice system. Thus, they might have also attempted to flee by changing their number and contact information, by hiding, by staying with family or friends, by changing their appearance, or by moving to a new location in order to get away from the stalker.[110] So after all attempts have been exhausted, victims often give up by learning to make do with the harm and to live in intense fear, which is sometimes described as "psychological terrorism."[111] Similar to the acquiescence or disassociation in domestic violence victims, stalking victims often "freeze" in a similar form of long term psychological paralysis.

Conclusion

Stalking is a crime like no other. Although Beck in *You* does not realize Joe is stalking her until it is too late, the first-person narrative novel delves into a hypermasculine stalker's psyche and his reasoning for choosing a hyperfeminine victim. The sexist influences that many stalkers like Joe use to justify

105 *Id.* at 324.

106 Laurie J. Tellefesen and Matthew B. Johnson, *False Victimization in Stalking: Clinical and Legal Aspects*, in 12.1 NYS Psychologist 20, 20 (2000).

107 See *People v. Gans* 52 Cal. App. 4th 147 (1997), a stalking case that explains that the "learned helplessness" occurs when "a woman or man is conditioned to believe that she/he cannot control what happens, and perception becomes reality" (147).

108 Collins and Wilkas, at 320.

109 *Id.*

110 Neal Miller, *Stalking Investigation, Law, Public Policy, and Criminal Prosecution as a Problem Solver*, in Stalking Crimes and Victim Protection: Prevention, Intervention, Threat Assessment, and Case Management 387, 401 (Joseph A. Davis, ed., 2001).

111 Claire Dalton and Elizabeth M. Schneider, *The Criminal Justice System* in Battered Women and the Law, 564, 575 (2001). See also Doris M. Hall, *The Victims of Stalking*, in The Psychology of Stalking: Clinical and Forensic Perspectives 113, 133 (J. Reid Meloy, ed., 1998).

their behavior can be traced back to traditional gender norms that reinforce masculine authority and feminine submissiveness. In this chapter, I argue that like sexual assault and domestic violence, these gender norms have negatively impacted the criminal justice system, and ultimately, the seriousness of stalking and these other crimes is dismissed. Since victims of long-term stalking rarely acquire help and support from the legal system, they typically do not have the means to fight or flee the stalker. I argue that as a result, through trauma and learned helplessness, victims remain frozen in perpetual fear. Without assistance from the criminal justice system, victims like the fictional Guinevere Beck and the real-life Rebecca Shaeffer may be relentlessly pursued by their stalkers to the point of murder.

5 Sexual Harassment

A Victim's Inaction Mistaken for Acquiescence in *The Boys Club* (2020)

Like sexual assault, domestic violence, and stalking, sexual harassment of women is based upon the age-old lie that "men are women's natural superiors" and that, as a result, they can treat women however they please.[1] Prior to 1975, sexual harassment did not exist. It was just a way of life—something primarily women had to endure from men in their workplace. Stemming from the "Mad Men" white, upper-middle-class culture of the 1950s and earlier, the predominating societal norm consisted of wives staying at home and caring for the household and children. Financially dependent, these women were under the sole discretion and authority of the breadwinning husbands. Therefore, the workplace—and the monetary success and freedom that came along with it—primarily belonged to men. So, for working women who began to assert independence and overstep these societal boundaries, many were subject to male objectification at best and abuse at worst. However, this behavior was part of the norm, and the women simply dealt with it. Nonetheless, although in current times that norm has been challenged thanks to the #MeToo movement, sexual harassment is still very common in many workplaces.[2] As feminist legal scholar Dr. Catherine A. MacKinnon puts it, sexual harassment is a form of sex discrimination in employment that "reinforces and expresses women's traditional and inferior role in the labor force."[3] Thus, in this chapter, I argue that like sexual assault and domestic abuse, sexual harassment of women has most often been permitted due to longstanding gender roles that reinforce toxic masculinity and excuse violence.

1 Catherine A. MacKinnon, Sexual Harassment of Working Women 4 (1979).

2 Matt Gonzales, *Five Years of #MeToo: Sexual Harassment Still Common in Workplaces*, SHRM: Better Workplaces Better World (Oct. 17, 2022), https://www.shrm.org/resourcesandtools/hr-topics/behavioral-competencies/global-and-cultural-effectiveness/pages/five-years-of-metoo-sexual-harassment-still-common-in-workplaces.aspx

3 MacKinnon, at 4.

DOI: 10.4324/9781003303572-5

Company Culture and Institutional Betrayal

Sexual harassment is not about sex. It is about perniciously leveraging authority and privilege in the workplace. It is about abusing a power differential between a person of higher rank and one of lower status. Sexual harassment goes on between men, women, and members of the LGBTQ+ community. However, according to the EEOC (Equal Opportunity Employment Commission), in the United States from the years 2018 to 2021, 78.2 percent of sexual harassment charges were filed by women.[4] Yet like allegations of sexual assault, most sexual harassment claims by victims go unreported.[5] Up until recently, one of the reasons for such a low percentage has been due to company policies that required recruits to sign a pre-employment NDA (Non-Disclosure Agreement).[6] Under these types of NDAs, employees were forced to seek arbitration, and it prohibited victims from publicly speaking about sexual harassment claims.[7] Since sexual harassment is not a crime, companies had the flexibility of an NDA of this nature.[8] Although now federal law prohibits forced arbitration, the longstanding practice has helped create a "veil of secrecy" and nontransparency that allows sexual harassers to continue perpetuating their abuse and "minimizes pressure on companies to fire predators."[9] The residual negative impact of forced arbitration combined with a sexist work environment contribute to abusers' ability to get away with sexual harassment.

Another way in which companies discredit sexual harassment victims and permit toxic behaviors is through its compromised culture. All strong organizations live by the merits of a company's value statement. By creating a value statement based on guidelines, ethical standards, and company policies, both large corporations and small businesses alike possess a good deal of discretion and authority.[10] Both the prescription and practice of "professional behavior"

4 U.S. Equal Employment Opportunity Commission, *Sexual Harassment in Our Nation's Workplaces,* EEOC Data Highlight (April 2022), https://www.eeoc.gov/sites/default/files/2022-04/Sexual%20Harassment%20Awareness%20Month%202022%20Data%20Highlight.pdf

5 *Id.*

6 Sharon O'Malley, *Workplace Sexual Harassment,* 27.38 CQ Press 893, 896 (2017).

7 *Id.*

8 According to Jennifer Freyd, "On March 3, 2022, President Joe Biden signed H.R. 4445 into law, which ensures that individuals (e.g. employees, customers, patients, and others) who have experienced sexual assault or sexual harassment cannot be forced into arbitration if they choose to litigate." However, the residuals of this longstanding toxic practice are still in place and continue to contribute to victims' unwillingness to report sexual harassment. Jennifer Freyd, *Resources for Changemakers,* Center for Institutional Courage, (updated March 2022), https://www.institutionalcourage.org/resources-for-changemakers

9 Gretchen Carlson, *Gretchen Carlson: How to Encourage More Women to Report Sexual Harassment,* The New York Times, (Oct. 10, 2017), https://tinyurl.com/yco7u6ww

10 Isaac H. Smith and Maryam Kouchaki, *Building an Ethical Company,* Harvard Business Review (Nov.–Dec. 2021), https://hbr.org/2021/11/building-an-ethical-company

are ultimately left up to each business and its corresponding organizational plan. However, a problem arises when criteria may be loosely defined, rarely enforced, or both. When the values are either weak or ignored, different forms of harmful conduct may arise, including sexual harassment. Thus, depending on the company's culture, if owners and executive leadership are not viewed as credible or moral, this can filter down to taint lower-level employees and negatively impact the business community.[11] Ultimately, there is no trustworthy organization if the leadership is not trustworthy.

When a company's culture lacks ethics, institutional betrayal may develop. According to psychologist Dr. Jennifer J. Freyd, institutional betrayal refers to "wrongdoings perpetuated by an institution upon individuals dependent on that institution."[12] This includes failure to "respond supportively" when victims are sexually harassed or assaulted.[13] A company, organization, or institution is supposed to shield those who depend on it against harm. However, when misconduct occurs within the institution and the organization refuses to assist those affected, the victims are betrayed while the perpetrators are protected. This concept sends a message that sexual harassment and other toxic behavior is permissible, and it encourages more violence.[14] Most often, sexual harassment victims are ignored, blamed, or even dismissed from their position within the company, and the offender goes unpunished. This is an example not only of institutional betrayal but also of institutional DARVO.

An aggressive form of institutional betrayal, institutional DARVO (Deny, Attack, Reverse Victim and Offender) occurs when an institution shifts blame from the offender to the victim.[15] DARVO is a common tactic used by sexual abusers, and it has been utilized by rapists, domestic violence perpetrators, stalkers, and harassers. A form of gaslighting, DARVO occurs when "the perpetrator or offender may Deny the behavior, Attack the individual doing the

11 According to Sharon O'Malley, "management's behavior is more important than policies," and "employees take their cues on what type of behavior is permitted." O'Malley, at 899.

12 Jennifer J. Freyd, *Institutional Betrayal and Institutional Courage,* UNIVERSITY OF OREGON, (7 Feb. 2023), https://dynamic.uoregon.edu/jjf/institutionalbetrayal/. Institutional betrayal is connected with Betrayal Trauma Theory. For more, see Jennifer J. Freyd, *The Psychology of Betrayal Trauma: Memory, Health, and Gender,* Thompson Hall Science and Mathematics Seminar at University of Puget Sound, Tacoma, WA (6 Mar. 2008); Melissa Platt, Jocelyn Barton, and Jennifer J. Freyd, *A Betrayal Trauma Perspective on Domestic Violence*, in VIOLENCE AGAINST WOMEN IN FAMILIES AND RELATIONSHIPS 201, 185 (2009); JENNIFER J. FREYD AND PAMELA BIRRELL, BLIND TO BETRAYAL: WHY WE FOOL OURSELVES WE AREN'T BEING FOOLED (2014).

13 Jennifer J. Freyd, *Institutional Betrayal and Institutional Courage,* UNIVERSITY OF OREGON, (7 Feb. 2023), https://dynamic.uoregon.edu/jjf/institutionalbetrayal/.

14 Jennifer M. Gomez and Jennifer J. Freyd, *Institutional Betrayal Makes Violence More Toxic,* THE REGISTER GUARD, A9 (22 Aug. 2014).

15 Jennifer J. Freyd, *What is DARVO?* UNIVERSITY OF OREGON, (7 Feb. 2023), https://dynamic.uoregon.edu/jjf/defineDARVO.html

confronting, and Reverse the roles of Victim and Offender so the perpetrator assumes the victim role and turns the true victim—or the whistle blower—into an alleged offender."[16] As a result, the abuser diminishes their wrongdoing and evades responsibility. Following in the footsteps of individuals who commit DARVO, institutional DARVO happens on an even larger scale and compounds trauma when the organization discredits and abandons the victim, as well.

Difficulty in Suing an Employer

When surveyed, 50 percent of women have been sexually harassed at work; however, only 5–15 percent of these women report the harassment to their employers for fear of retaliation.[17] Of those who report the harassment and file a legal claim, only 3–6 percent of these cases ever make it to trial.[18] The reason for such a low percentage is because in general, harassment laws favor the employer. Of the few claims that are reported, most are either dismissed or settled out of court. In addition, suing an employer is stressful, time-consuming, emotionally taxing, and extremely expensive.[19] What many employees fail to realize is that just because an employer treats someone inconsiderately, unfairly, or obtusely does not necessarily mean that the employer violated the law.[20] Employees also tend not to understand that their employers are typically undeterred by the possibility of litigation, and even if the employee "wins," not much will change.[21] Also, hiring an attorney who specializes in labor law is a costly, necessary requirement, and most lawyers are very selective due to the low success rate. Explaining this concept, Cincinnati employment attorney Randy Freking says that he only takes on cases "worth a shot at winning and warns clients that even the strongest cases have a good chance at getting dismissed."[22] Therefore, although federal laws are in place to prevent sexual harassment in the workplace, these laws rarely serve the victims they are supposed to protect.

16 *Id.*

17 Yuki Noguchi, *Sexual Harassment Cases Often Rejected by Courts*, NPR (Nov. 28, 2017), https://www.npr.org/2017/11/28/565743374/sexual-harassment-cases-often-rejected-by-courts

18 *Id.*

19 Anderson Hunter Law Firm, *Should You Sue Your Employer? 11 Things to Consider*, Employment Law, Mediation, and Public Contracts (Feb. 24, 2022), https://andersonhunterlaw.com/blog/should-sue-your-employer

20 Robin Shea, *Before You Sue: 10 Questions Every Employee Should Ask*, Employment and Labor Insider: Legalese Not Spoken Here (Nov. 20, 2015), https://www.constangy.com/employment-labor-insider/before-you-sue-10-questions-every-employee-should-ask

21 *Id.*

22 See Yuki Noguchi.

Sexual Harassment Law

Workplace sexual harassment is a form of gender discrimination that is prohibited by Title VII of the 1964 Civil Rights Act.[23] It includes "unwelcome sexual advances, requests for sexual favors, or other forms of physical or verbal harassment."[24] It also encompasses offensive remarks about a person's gender, even if the comments are not sexual in nature.[25] Under Title VII, the victim and the harasser may be of any gender, and this law also covers members of the gay, lesbian, and transgender communities.[26] Before filing a lawsuit, federal law requires the victim to exhaust all administrative possibilities first. For example, she must inform the company's human resources department in writing, and if the company does not take any action to resolve the issue, the victim may move forward with legal action. This means that she must then file a claim with the EEOC and corresponding state agency. In turn, the EEOC may require the employer to change its work policies, it may file a lawsuit on the victim's behalf, or it may choose not to intervene but rather allow the victim to file a civil lawsuit on their own.[27]

According to *Meritor Savings Bank v. Vinson* (1986) there are two forms of sexual harassment under Title VII: either "quid pro quo" or "hostile work environment."[28] The most common form of sexual harassment, a hostile work environment claim requires the plaintiff to demonstrate that "the harassment was so pervasive that it negatively impacted the victim's ability to perform her job functions."[29] According to *Hunt v. Wal-Mart Stores, Inc.* (2019), plaintiffs must show that "1) the work environment was subjectively and objectively offensive; 2) the harassment was based on gender; 3) the conduct was either severe or pervasive; 4) there is a basis for employer liability."[30] Under these legal elements, a victim typically has difficulty in proving intentional, "severe or pervasive conduct" because in most hostile work environment claims, the court requires the plaintiff to demonstrate that the harassment occurred

23 Sharon O'Malley, *Workplace Sexual Harassment,* 27.38 CQ Press 896, 893 (2017).

24 U.S. Equal Employment Opportunity Commission, *Sexual Harassment*, https://www.eeoc.gov/sexual-harassment#:~:text=It%20is%20unlawful%20to%20harass,harassment%20of%20a%20sexual%20nature.

25 *Id.*

26 *Id.*

27 U.S. Equal Employment Opportunity Commission, *Filing a Lawsuit,* https://www.eeoc.gov/filing-lawsuit *Meritor Savings Bank v. Venison* 477 U.S. 57 (1986). *See also EEOC v. Central Wholesalers, Inc.* 573 F.3d 167 (4th Cir. 2009).

28 *Id.*

29 *Hunt v. Wal-Mart Stores, Inc.* No. 18-3403 (7th Cir. 2019), *aff'd.* On July 26, 2019, the 7th circuit affirmed the district court's summary judgment on the Title VII sexual harassment hostile environment claim.

30 *Id.*

multiple times through a series of events.[31] Specifically, as stated in *Clark County School District v. Breeden* (2001), the court reviews the "frequency of the discriminatory conduct" that occurs over time.[32] In other words, one incident of sexual harassment is not usually legally actionable.[33]

In addition, another reason why so few cases favor the victim is because many may be dismissed because the employer adopted and distributed a policy.[34] This concept derives from the Supreme Court decision *Faragher v. City of Boca Raton* (1998), which gives employers a defense against sexual harassment claims so long as the employer took reasonable measures to prevent and correct the harassment through internal complaint procedures, and the victim failed to utilize those mechanisms.[35] Furthermore, in *Leopold v. Baccarat, Inc.* (2001), the New York appellate court noted that even if the company policy is inadequate, "the law is very clear that any reasonable policy will do."[36] In other words, an employer most often satisfies the defense of liability by having a policy in place, and the courts do not require the employer to take "strong disciplinary action against the harasser."[37] As sociologist Dr. Lauren Edelman puts it, "courts have become complicit in this development, crediting employers for superficial procedures without assessing whether they actually work."[38] This is not only a reason as to why harassers continue to harass but also why victims continue to experience institutional DARVO from both the employer and the legal system.

In contrast to hostile work environment, quid pro quo sexual harassment claims must demonstrate that an employer required an employee to provide

31 Debra S. Katz, *Sexual Harassment Claims and Defenses in Federal Court* in Katz, Marshall, and Banks, LLP (2011). https://katzbanks.com/wp-content/uploads/110214-CLE-Katz-Sexual-Harassment-Federal-Claims-Defenses.pdf Katz mentions that "the courts have generally been reluctant to allow [single-incident claims], except where that single incident was so severe, such as an extreme physical assault or truly egregious verbal threats, that the incident materially altered the conditions of their employment." See also *Harris v. Forklift Systems, Inc.* (1993), which states that in order to prove whether an environment is "hostile" or "abusive," may include "the frequency of the discriminatory conduct; its severity; whether it is physically threatening or humiliating, or a more offensive utterance; and whether it unreasonably interferes with an employee's work performance" 510 U.S. 17, 21–22 (1993).

32 *Clark County School District v. Breeden,* 532 U.S. 268 (2001).

33 *Id.* See also *Faragher v. City of Boca Raton* (1998), which states that "simple teasing, offhand comments, or isolated incidents (unless extremely serious) will not amount to discriminatory changes in the 'terms and conditions of employment'." 524 U.S. 775, 788 (1998).

34 Elizabeth C. Tippet, *Employers Handle Sexual Harassment as a Business Decision in* Gale Opposing Viewpoints Online Collection (2017), https://go-gale-com.dcccd.idm.oclc.org/ps/i.do?p=OVIC&u=txshracd2500&id=GALE%7CFKESQV562085954&v=2.1&it=r&aty=ip

35 *Faragher v. City of Boca Raton*, 524 U.S. 775 (1998).

36 *Leopold v. Baccarat, Inc.* 174 F.3d 261 (2d Cir. 2001), *aff'd.*

37 Tippet.

38 Lauren B. Edelman and Jessica Cabrera, *Sex-Based Harassment and Symbolic Compliance in* 16 Ann. Rev. of Law and Social Science, 361, 361 (2020).

sexual favors in exchange for a work benefit or to prevent the employee from receiving a negative job action. According to *LeGrand v. Area Resources for Community and Human Services* (2005), "a plaintiff must show 1) membership of a protected group; 2) subjection to unwelcome sexual harassment; 3) the harassment was severe and pervasive and resulted in creating a hostile work environment."[39] However, unlike the more common hostile work environment claims, a quid pro quo claim does not require multiple incidents to occur in order to prove "severe and pervasive" conduct.[40] Instead, the plaintiff must prove that the sexual advance(s) toward her were "unwelcomed."[41] In addition, since Title VII does not prohibit "all verbal or physical harassment in the workplace," the victim must prove that the discrimination was connected to gender bias.[42] Under these legal elements, plaintiffs sometimes have difficulty proving "unwelcomeness" when the defendant can demonstrate either denial by stating "it didn't happen" or that it was consensual and therefore "welcomed." To that end, when it becomes one word against the other, the burden of proof under the preponderance of evidence standard will most often not be met.

The Boys Club (2021) and Sexual Harassment: A Culture of Complicity

Despite the increased social awareness created by the #MeToo movement, in certain fields, businesses, or workplaces, sexual harassment is still a pervasive issue that revolves around a predominating culture of complicity. Set in the current time, Erica Katz's novel *The Boys Club* (2020) illustrates an example of a competitive, high-stakes work environment and a corporate culture that is dominated by sexism. The book provides a narrative that demonstrates the ease by which sexual harassment may occur in the workplace, especially between young, inexperienced female law associates and their older male supervising attorneys, who have the authority to either promote or demote them. These women must play by the rules of a hierarchal gendered structure designed for men to stay on top and possess all the power and authority. In exchange for a seat at the table, the women endure being sexually harassed, feel pressured to have affairs with their superiors, or both. Under the most extreme circumstances, they are expected to stay quiet after being sexually assaulted.

39 *LeGrand v. Area Resources for Community and Human Services*, 394 F.3d 1098, 1102 (8th Cir. 2004).

40 *See Lutkewitte v. Gonzales*, 436 F.3d 248 (D.C. Cir. 2006).

41 *EEOC v. Prospect Airport Services, Inc.*, 621 F3D. 991, 997-998 (9th Cir. 2010).

42 *Oncale v. Sundowner Offshore Services, Inc.*, U.S. 75, 80 (1998).

Along with sexual harassment, *The Boys Club* highlights materialism and the power of American capitalism, wealth, masculine privilege, and beauty bias. The novel's characters dress to impress and brag about the expensive clothing brands they wear. They spend an excessive amount of money showing off through fine dining, heavy partying, and entertaining clients. The most successful and well-revered consist of a select, all-male group of attorneys in the Mergers and Acquisitions (M & A) specialty. However trite, the novel's superficialities reinforce real-world aspects of society that are part of the status quo and that are much more dominant than the audience may either realize or choose to admit. Ultimately, by the end, the book answers the big question based on the mistaken belief: why would a woman "allow" herself to be sexually harassed?

The Boys Club is told in first-person narrative by the main character, Alexandra (Alex) Vogel. A Harvard Law School graduate, Alex is smart, successful, and fully capable; however, she downplays her achievements due to her youth, inexperience, and insecurities. The novel begins with her first day as a new associate at the "BigLaw" law firm in New York City, Klasko & Fitch. As the story unfolds, Alex competes to "match" with a specialty and seal her long-term employment with the firm. Over the course of nine months, she becomes immersed in the company culture of overwork, materialism, and cutthroat rivalry. Alex is also exposed to gender-biased slurs, objectification toward herself and other females, improper sexual exchanges, and other forms of sexual harassment as she simultaneously works hard to achieve a coveted spot in the M & A group, "The Boys Club."

The Acceptance of Toxic Masculinity in the Workplace

As I argue in previous chapters, mainstream society often idealizes hypermasculine men—those who exaggerate certain stereotypical characteristics that suggest strength, dominance, and leadership. Specifically, four characteristics that are associated with hypermasculine men are "1) the view that violence is a form of 'manliness;' 2) the perspective that danger is exciting; 3) a behavior of callousness toward women; and 4) a disdain toward 'emotional displays' that are considered 'feminine'."[43] Exemplifying "callousness toward women," the notorious M & A group in *The Boys Club* is described as "a bunch of frat boys who walk around like they own this place."[44] A female real estate partner warns Alex that they "don't let women in. They say they try to promote women, and it's the hours that weed them out. But it's their attitudes.

43 Ronald O. Craig, *Definition: Hypermasculinity*, Britannica (Jan. 2, 2019), https://www.britannica.com/topic/hypermasculinity

44 Katz, at 39.

Misogynists, all of them."[45] In this case, the M & A group embodies Klasko & Fitch's corporate structure where "masculine ideals warp into culture," creating a "fertile ground for the proliferation of toxic leadership."[46] Characterized by abusive strategies, this form of leadership is designed to control and bully other employees.[47] When male supervisors command and manipulate female employees through harassment, this nefarious leadership style normalizes toxic masculinity—men use their hypermasculine traits as an excuse for abuse and violence toward women.

The Acceptance of Sexual Harassment in the Workplace

Throughout *The Boys Club,* the audience witnesses several different types of sexual harassment during Alex's nine-month journey with the M & A group. First, the audience becomes exposed to the general acceptance of sexual harassment as part of the culture. Alex is expected to tolerate disparaging remarks and gender-based degradation not only toward herself but also toward other female employees. As the story continues, the audience witnesses her grooming by Peter Dunn, an attractive partner of the M & A group. And finally, the audience observes the most pernicious form of harassment when she is first groped and then almost sexually assaulted by a wealthy client, Gary Kaplan. When Alex tries to seek help from superiors after the first incident with Mr. Kaplan, all of them dismiss his "bad behavior" and she is expected to tolerate it. As a result, she does not report the attempted sexual assault because she knows no one will help her.

While not all the men in the M & A group sexually harass Alex, they implicitly condone the slurs, degrading remarks, affairs, and fondling directed at female associates at Klasko & Fitch. The group chooses to allow her to work with them because of her agreeableness and gullibility; she is perceived as an "attractive, well-behaved, goody two-shoes woman" who has been socially conditioned to be amenable and polite.[48] An only child of wealthy parents, Alex has also been spoiled and sheltered. However, like most smart, driven, young people who enter the workforce right out of law school, she is still trying to figure out who she is as an adult and a professional, and she lacks experience, life skills, and self-sufficiency. She naively values the superficiality of materialism and the appearance of success: "I wanted this life,

45 *Id.* at 40.

46 Kenneth Matos, Olivia (Mandy) O'Neil, and Xue Lei, *Toxic Leadership and the Masculinity Contest: How "Win or Die" Cultures Breed Abusive Leadership,* 74.3 Journal of Social Issues 500, 501 (2018). See also Jennifer J. Berdal et al., *Work as a Masculinity Contest,* 74.3 Journal of Social Issues 422, 422 (2018).

47 *Id.*

48 Katz, at 100.

my luxurious apartment, a wardrobe full of new clothes."[49] Additionally, she possesses an unrealistic view of what it means to work as an associate attorney in a "BigLaw" firm: Alex feels like she's "playing a lawyer on TV" and is starstruck with the idea.[50] She is also starstruck with the wealthy firm and the benefits she acquires: "offices with unobstructed views of Manhattan," firm cell phones, laptops, credit cards, 401ks, health insurance, memberships, and after-work happy hours."[51] However, despite these benefits, Alex admits to having Imposter's Syndrome, and she feels inferior to her peers.[52] So although she is a smart, industrious young woman, her lack of confidence and experience leaves her vulnerable to exploitation and abuse. The M & A group recognizes this and knows she is easy to manipulate.

Psychoemotional Vulnerabilities in the Sexual Harassment Victim

According to psychologist Dr. Grant Sinnamon, certain "psychoemotional vulnerabilities" make victims more susceptible to grooming, sexual harassment, and other forms of abuse.[53] Perpetrators typically target victims with distinguishing qualities because they perceive these victims as easy to control.[54] Specifically, these characteristics include desire, low self-esteem, age, cultural factors, and avoidance.[55] Possessing these qualities, Alex and other young women in the law firm become prime targets for harassment. For example, Alex possesses desire in that she wants to stand out and be different from her peers. To accomplish this task, she vows to do more and work harder than anyone else.[56] Due to Alex's age and lack of experience, she does not necessarily possess low self-esteem, but rather she is insecure and self-critical. She compensates for her insecurity by being "a people pleaser," who "forces a smile" even when she is being treated poorly.[57] As the novel progresses, she copes with avoidance and convinces herself that everything is fine. However, her physical, mental, and emotional health are deteriorating, and her personal relationships become strained. Although she becomes exhausted from overwork, she puts on a front that her life is perfect. Due to her youth and naivete,

49 *Id.* at 11.
50 *Id.* at 22.
51 *Id.* at 26.
52 *Id.* at 24.
53 Grant Sinnamon *Ch. 16: The Psychology of Adult Grooming: Sinnamon's Seven-Stage Model of Adult Grooming*, in The Psychology of Criminal and Antisocial Behavior: Victim and Offender Perspectives, 462, 459 (Wayne Petherick and Grant Sinnamon, eds., 2017).
54 *Id.*
55 Sinnamon, at 468–470.
56 Katz, at 92.
57 *Id.* at 140.

she is also easily influenced by those she admires. Specifically, Alex becomes enchanted when the handsome, married partner Peter Dunn pays special attention to her. She describes her instant attraction as "suddenly [being] overcome by the desire to be in [his] line of vision—to remind him I existed."[58]

Possessing these characteristics increases victims' likelihood of being abused. In this case, the most prominent psychoemotional vulnerability Alex possesses is her use of avoidance when faced with difficult circumstances. Using avoidance as a coping mechanism "involves cognitive and behavioral efforts oriented toward denying, minimizing, or otherwise avoiding dealing directly with stressful demands."[59] An example of Alex's avoidance arises when she is first invited to dinner with an M & A client who says "I didn't think you'd look like this" while looking her up and down.[60] Alex feels immediately annoyed but dismisses her gut reaction.[61] She sells herself out and instead begins to flirt with him, hoping to please her senior attorneys. When the client goes on to talk about a female analyst's unattractive physical qualities, Alex continues to feel uncomfortable with his objectification of women. She quickly realizes that her presence as the only female attorney amongst the men is a "test of sorts" to "keep the client entertained."[62] However, she "shoves the feeling that I was somehow betraying my own sex out of my mind. It was all too easily replaced by the sweetness of inclusion."[63] To Alex, even though her gut reaction is the correct one, she rationalizes it away for the sake of belonging.

Another time Alex uses avoidance occurs when a group of male attorneys and another M & A client compare Alex to her co-worker, Carmen. The client tells Alex that while she is "hot in a way that makes everybody want to take care of her," her friend Carmen is hot "in a way that makes you want to treat her like shit."[64] Although Alex feels offended and recognizes she is being denigrated, she explains that "it didn't feel like harassment. It felt like a compliment."[65] In this case, Alex uses avoidance to justify being harassed because she needs to be liked by clients. To her, above all, she wants "positive performance reviews," for "a smoother path to success."[66] Thus,

58 *Id.* at 84.

59 R.C. Cronkite, et al., *Life Circumstances and Personal Resources as Predictors of the 10-Year Course of Depression in* American Journal of Community Psychology, 26. 255, 255 (1998). See also J. A. Penley, J. Tomaka, and J. S. Wiebe, *The Association of Coping to Physical and Psychological Health Outcomes: A Meta-Analytic Review in* Journal of Behavioral Medicine, 6.551, 551 (2002).

60 *Id.* at 94.

61 *Id.* at 94.

62 *Id.* at 99.

63 *Id.* at 95.

64 *Id.* at 105.

65 *Id.* at 105.

66 *Id.* at 105.

she ultimately views her harassment not only as a necessary evil but also as something she cannot escape: "I could either accept [the] behavior as an insult or accept it as a challenge. But either way, I had to accept it."[67]

Adult Grooming in the Workplace

Due to her psychoemotional vulnerabilities and a toxic work environment, Alex becomes prone to sexual harassment by clients and employees; however, she also is prone to being groomed by the older and more experienced M & A partner, Peter Dunn. According to scholars Georgia M. Winters and Elizabeth L. Jeglic, in many sexual harassment cases, the perpetrators groom their adult victims.[68] Predators use specific tactics over the course of weeks, months, or even years. They use manipulative emotional and psychological maneuvers that target a vulnerable victim to "prepare a person for sexual exploitation and/or abuse."[69] Even though most research on grooming has been conducted with respect to child sexual abuse, anyone can be groomed. As author and sex counselor Eric Marlowe Goodson puts it, "Grooming is the slow, methodical, and intentional process of manipulating a person to a point where they can be victimized."[70] Perpetrators target victims who they view as vulnerable, insecure, gullible, or naïve, and then they begin to build trust.[71] Sexual harassers leverage their authority to surreptitiously exploit victims to have sexual encounters with them. In Alex's case, Peter Dunn grooms her, and she eventually has an affair with him.

The Characteristics of a Sexual Predator-Groomer and *The Boys Club*

In *The Psychology of Adult Grooming* (2017), author and psychologist Dr. Grant Sinnamon states that the "personal power" characteristics of a sexual predator include "notoriety, charisma and charm, social status, and personal standing."[72] Particularly in sexual harassment cases, the groomer looks for

67 *Id.* at 113.

68 Georgia M. Winters and Elizabeth L. Jeglic, *Adults in Sexual Grooming*, in SEXUAL GROOMING: INTEGRATING RESEARCH, PRACTICE, PREVENTION, AND POLICY 177, 177 (2022).

69 GRANT SINNAMON *Ch. 16: The Psychology of Adult Grooming: Sinnamon's Seven-Stage Model of Adult Grooming*, in THE PSYCHOLOGY OF CRIMINAL AND ANTISOCIAL BEHAVIOR: VICTIM AND OFFENDER PERSPECTIVES, 462, 459 (Wayne Petherick and Grant Sinnamon, eds., 2017).

70 Emma Sarran Webster, *What is Sexual Grooming? 7 Things to Know About This Tactic,* ALLURE (July 19, 2017, https://www.allure.com/story/what-is-sexual-grooming-abuse).

71 Webster.

72 GRANT SINNAMON *Ch. 16: The Psychology of Adult Grooming: Sinnamon's Seven-Stage Model of Adult Grooming*, in THE PSYCHOLOGY OF CRIMINAL AND ANTISOCIAL BEHAVIOR: VICTIM AND OFFENDER PERSPECTIVES, 460, 466–468 (Wayne Petherick and Grant Sinnamon, eds., 2017).

ways to gain the victim's favor by emphasizing his own influence.[73] He uses his wealth, good looks, and authority to manipulate the victim into thinking she is "special" to him. For example, Peter Dunn uses his notoriety to impress Alex when they meet outside of work for the first time. He takes her to an oyster bar, and even though it is closing time, the manager keeps the restaurant open just for him. Bewildered, Alex ponders if anyone ever "says no to this man?"[74] In this sense, from the beginning, Peter flatters Alex and makes her feel exceptional. Due to her insecurities, she becomes bewildered by his infamy, and she cannot believe that he would give her special attention. In this case, grooming begins with what appears to be a friendship, and it can often be mistaken for a budding romance.[75]

Sinnamon's Seven Stage Model of Adult Grooming

Groomers such as Peter Dunn use favors, promises, and attentiveness to initially gain trust, and they choose victims who are typically young, inexperienced, and susceptible to criticism, persuasion, and temptation.[76] According to Dr. Grant Sinnamon's Seven Stage Model of Adult Grooming, a perpetrator prepares the victim for sexual contact in the first five stages, and he exploits the victim in order to continue the sexual contact in the final two stages.[77] In the first stage, abusers often take advantage of a "hunting ground environment" and select victims who are assailable.[78] Along with Alex's predisposed traits and psychoemotional vulnerabilities, she also does not have much of a support network outside of her parents and boyfriend. Unlike many of the new first-year associates at the law firm, Alex does not have friends from law school or college who work there.[79] Instead, she is alone and becomes a prime target for Peter's grooming. This isolation contributes to Peter's second phase of preparation—he gathers information about her to target her needs and susceptibilities.[80] For example, after a few months, Alex learns that the M & A group capitalizes on her reputation as being a "wholesome" people-pleaser. Peter says that "all of the partners identify [the new junior associates] by an adjective for convenience's sake."[81] He goes on to explain that Alex is known as "prissy, proper, perfect, [and] ready for the country club."[82] Peter divulges

73 Webster.
74 Katz, at 120.
75 Webster.
76 *Id.*
77 Sinnamon, at 475.
78 *Id.* at 475.
79 Katz, at 77.
80 Sinnamon, at 476.
81 Katz, at 239.
82 *Id.*

this covert information to flatter her and to begin to form an intimate bond. He uses this tactic and others to progress to stage three of Sinnamon's Model where the predator establishes a sense of trust by finding ways in which he can insert himself into the victim's life.[83] In this stage, Peter works to exploit vulnerabilities by creating false intimacy. He "blurs the lines between what is appropriate," and he creates "secrets" and "special" moments.[84] In the novel, Peter takes advantage of Alex's mental and emotional strain as she works longer hours at the firm due to her increasingly demanding schedule. For example, after a grueling set of conference calls that last over four hours, Alex is taken off guard when "Peter gave a small smile as if we shared a secret, and I smiled back, though not understanding what it might be."[85]

After establishing and continuing a bond of false intimacy, Peter moves on to the fourth stage of Sinnamon's Model—Meeting the Need and Establishing Credentials.[86] In this stage, "the predator secures their credibility by exploiting the information they have" to "fulfill the identified need in their target."[87] Peter identifies Alex's need to be recognized by him and to succeed at the firm, and he manufactures scenarios so he can further establish personal connections. An example of one scenario includes Peter's first "chance" encounter with Alex at a gathering at a restaurant with her and a few of the first-year associates. He suddenly shows up to greet Alex in front of her colleagues. At the time, Alex does not realize that the partners have access to all firm emails and texts on the firm's cell phones. So, Peter can stalk her, track her whereabouts, and confirm her plans. When he "meets" her at the restaurant, he quickly establishes his credibility by directly acknowledging her. As a result, her associates are impressed, and Alex feels special. His attention also escalates to intentional physical contact when Alex describes that, "Peter put a steady palm on my shoulder and turned to leave, then allowed his hand to linger for a moment behind him … [and] my pulse almost stopped."[88]

As the sexual energy develops between them over the course of a few weeks, Peter progresses to stage five—Priming the Target.[89] In this stage, the predator uses his established personal connection with the victim and begins to isolate her from friends and family "who may threaten [his] plans."[90] In this case, Peter does not have to work hard to isolate Alex since she already spends most of her waking hours at the firm, and she is there seven days a week.[91]

83 Sinnamon, at 478.
84 *Id.* at 478.
85 Katz, at 114.
86 Sinnamon, at 478.
87 *Id.* at 474.
88 Katz, at 82.
89 Sinnamon, at 479.
90 *Id.*
91 Katz, at 125.

This explains how the lines become blurred between work colleagues and friends. Since the lawyers put in long hours, they often "do what friends do" by going to lunches, dinners, happy hours, retreats, and other activities funded by the law firm.[92] Peter uses this to his advantage to continue to create a false sense of intimacy with Alex.

After the tension continues to build, Peter instigates sexual contact—which is stage six of Sinnamon's Model.[93] In this stage, the predator uses the target's vulnerabilities "to exploit their weaknesses and instigate full-blown sexual contact."[94] The victim becomes "entangled in a sexually exploitative relationship."[95] For example, Peter lures a willing Alex away from the firm's holiday party to his car, and they have sex. Their behavior is flagrant and risky as both have attended the party with their significant others. A week after the holiday party, they have sex again when Peter visits Alex in their office. Experiencing conflicting emotions of lust and guilt, Alex feels jealous of Peter's wife. Also, Peter is emotionally unavailable—which makes Alex want him even more. Alex ultimately feels powerless against Peter and believes he has "complete control" over her.[96]

Knowing this, Peter initiates the seventh stage of Sinnamon's Model of Adult Grooming—Controlling the Victim.[97] Here, the predator controls the victim through "secrecy, guilt, blame, threat, bribery or promises of reward."[98] In this case, while Peter does not necessarily threaten, bribe, or promise a reward, he manipulates Alex through "secrecy, guilt, and blame" because he understands that Alex does not want anyone at the firm to know that she is sleeping with a partner. He also understands that she feels shame for cheating on her boyfriend, and he uses her guilt to his advantage. For example, after they have sex a second time, Peter manipulates Alex by then removing his affections, and he ignores her. Over the next week, she only hears from him about work. His emotional unavailability creates a power dynamic by which he controls their intimacy, and she in turn feels helpless. At this point, Alex has become entangled in an exploitive affair with one of the most powerful partners at her law firm who could make or break her entire career.

92 *Id.* at 74.
93 SINNAMON, at 480.
94 *Id.* at 474.
95 *Id.* at 474.
96 KATZ, at 257.
97 SINNAMON, at 481.
98 *Id.* at 474.

"Consensual" Affairs and *The Boys Club*

Towards the end of the novel, the audience learns that "consensual" affairs between higher and lower-ranking employees frequently occur at the Klasko & Fitch law firm. Since men hold most of the superior positions, many of these men have affairs with female subordinates. According to Catherine MacKinnon, affairs between two people with a power differential, where one is superior and the other is inferior, are common and may even be considered "normative."[99] However, what makes this sexual harassment is the power differential.[100] The superior party can "exploit the rights" and "deny the choice" of the inferior party."[101] At the end of the novel, the audience learns that Peter Dunn has been having "consensual" affairs with many lower-ranking women for a long period of time.[102] Alex ultimately finds out that he was sleeping with a fellow first-year attorney, Carmen, at the same time he was sleeping with her. When both women make this discovery, Carmen explains they were sexually harassed and could not technically consent due to the power differential: "First of all, partners can't sleep with associates. Second, what does 'consent' even mean when the power dynamic is so screwed up?"[103] To further prove the point about not being able to consent, Carmen asks Alex to consider what would happen "if you had turned him down? Or tried to end it? It's sexual harassment if you even need to think about those things."[104]

Sexual Harassment and Assault and the "Freeze" Response

Over the course of the months that Alex works at Klasko & Fitch's M & A department, she is sexually harassed not only by a partner but also by a client of the law firm. However, unlike the attractive, charming Peter Dunn who grooms and manipulates Alex into having an affair, Gary Kaplan is very different. From the beginning of the novel, Alex feels repulsed by M & A's wealthiest client. She does not like to meet with him because of his blatant sexism and misogynistic slurs. However, like Peter Dunn, Gary also accesses firm calendars and emails and "shows up" one day at a restaurant where she

99 Catherine A. MacKinnon, *Sexual Harassment: The Law, the Politics, and the Movement*, YouTube, UMich Donia Human Rights Center (April 15, 2019), https://www.google.com/search?q=katherine+mackinnon+sexual+harassment&sxsrf=APwXEdeUqr4a3OuodK2UPtf_fXEnyWTVSg:1682703781229&source=lnms&tbm=vid&sa=X&ved=2ahUKEwisq5GJkM3-AhVjnGoFHZmxCDEQ0pQJegQIBxAG&biw=1223&bih=662&dpr=2#fpstate=ive&vld=cid:d44bff25,vid:0MIQfjFf5Gc

100 *Id.*

101 *Id.*

102 Katz, at 353.

103 *Id.* at 358.

104 *Id.* at 358.

is celebrating with her family. In this instance, Alex finds Gary and an unidentified female in the rest room at the restaurant, and they have just had sex. Shocked and disgusted, Alex admits that he makes her skin crawl and he "chills her spine."[105] However, she ultimately puts up with him because "he is the firm's best client."[106]

Shortly after the incident, Gary's behavior progresses from sexist comments and inappropriate encounters to groping Alex. At the formal Stag River gala, he brazenly grabs her breast while she reaches over to put food from the buffet on her plate.[107] Alex immediately believes it is a mistake and she apologizes.[108] However, he simply replies, "please don't apologize," and assaults her again by placing his hand above her heart and reaching in to stroke her breast beneath her strapless dress.[109] At that time, she "froze" and "couldn't manage to move [her] legs to escape.[110] She feels so traumatized that she doubts herself: "It was the most unexpected, most disturbing thing to ever happen to me, and the fact that it happened so flagrantly, with my colleagues all around, made me question whether it happened at all."[111]

In this case, Alex experiences the "freeze" response when Gary violates her. As discussed in previous chapters, the acute freeze response commonly occurs when victims are sexually assaulted, stalked, or subjected to domestic violence. According to psychologist Dr. Jim Hopper, freezing not only happens during sexual assault but also in "incidents of severe sexual harassment."[112] When a victim freezes, "the brain's defense circuitry" stops all movement, and "there are no behaviors to choose from."[113] Later, "when victims attempt to understand and explain what happened," survivors like Alex often say things like "I was in shock," "I froze," or "All I could think was …"[114] Alex's reaction exemplifies these characteristics of the freeze response, and she is so stunned that she questions whether it actually happened.[115] She

105 *Id.* at 134.

106 *Id.*

107 *Id.* at 184.

108 *Id.*

109 *Id.*

110 *Id.*

111 *Id.* at 185.

112 Jim Hopper, *Freezing During Sexual Assault and Harassment*, in PSYCHOLOGY TODAY (Apr. 3, 2018), https://www.psychologytoday.com/us/blog/sexual-assault-and-the-brain/201804/freezing-during-sexual-assault-and-harassment#:~:text=Freezing%20happens%20in%20many%20sexual,effects%20on%20experience%20and%20behavior.

113 *Id.*

114 *Id.*

115 According to the University of Milwaukee Student Health and Wellness Center, some common reactions to sexual assault include "shock, disbelief, and denial." *What Are the Common Reactions to Sexual Assault?* (2023): https://uwm.edu/wellness/qa_faqs/what-are-common-reactions-to-sexual-assault/

also automatically begins to blame herself, which is another common reaction to this type of trauma.[116] She explains that although she thought her dress "was modest," she questions whether instead it made her "look like a slut?"[117] She also ponders whether she applied too much makeup that made her look sexually "easy": "I shouldn't have worn lip gloss. Or maybe the eyeliner was too heavy?"[118] In this instance, Alex not only blames herself for being assaulted but also engages in the same of type sexism as her harassers. By defaulting to "promiscuity stereotypes" against women, she criticizes herself for not being worthy of respect due to her manner of dress and appearance. In reality, regardless of what Alex wears, she is not to blame for being sexually harassed and assaulted.

Sexual Harassment, Victim Blame, and PTSD

Like some survivors, Alex mistakenly believes that she will acquire assistance and support from her supervisors after she reports Gary Kaplan's harassment. Instead, she discovers that they excuse his behavior and even blame her for "being difficult." When she talks to her supervising attorney, Jordan Sellar, about the incident, he shocks her by replying "If I had tits, I'd let him grab them both."[119] With this comment, Alex experiences secondary trauma not only from Jordan's dismissal but also from his response, which contains sexual harassment. This is the first time Alex witnesses the reality of "The Boys Club" and realizes that she is not safe. Her male colleagues in the M & A group have been feigning protection to manipulate her. In fact, some are capable of being just as sexist and perhaps as dangerous as Gary Kaplan himself.

Even after Alex tells Vivienne White, her female partner-mentor, Vivienne dismisses it completely: "He's so grabby."[120] Instead, she recommends that Alex go to the next gala where Gary will be in attendance because it will "show [Alex's] status in the M & A group."[121] Explaining that "it's out of [her] hands," Vivienne suggests Alex "stick it out" until match day because after that time, she can decline Gary's invitations.[122] According to Dr. Catherine MacKinnon, when a woman goes to another woman about sexual harassment and she dismisses it, the main reason is because the woman is accountable to a

116 Sadie Larsen and Louise Fitzgerald, *PTSD Symptoms and Sexual Harassment: The Role of Attributions and Perceived Control*, in JOURNAL OF INTERPERSONAL VIOLENCE 2, 1 (2010).

117 KATZ, at 185.

118 *Id.* at 185.

119 *Id.*

120 *Id.*

121 *Id.*

122 *Id.*

powerful man, and that man is backing her up.[123] Although we might expect a woman in a powerful position to be empathetic, the opposite often occurs due to the power dynamic and hierarchal nature of the corporate structure.[124] That dynamic rests on the highest level of leadership, which ultimately establishes the business culture. In this case, Vivienne White answers to other men who have helped establish and further support sexism in the workplace. If she subverts the recognized toxic, sexist norm, she will most likely be fired.

When Alex tries to bring the incident back up one more time with Jordan a few weeks later, he even more boldly informs her of the "rules." He reminds her that she is one of the few women in the M & A group and, "When you're a boss, you can make your own rules. For now, all the young people, men and women, just need to take the shit they're given."[125] With that, although she is upset, she uses her coping mechanism of avoidance to convince herself that making it in the M & A group supersedes everything else—even being sexually harassed and assaulted. She then gives up and diverts her attention to the expensive hotels, the Rolls Royce she travels in, and the coveted inclusivity of being part of such an elite group. To further disassociate and cope with both her trauma and the stressful work schedule, she also tries cocaine for the first time and begins to use alcohol and drugs more frequently.

When her supervisors ignore her request for help from being harassed, Gary's behavior dangerously escalates, and he attempts to rape her. This occurs after Alex takes Vivienne White's advice and attends the next gala. Although Alex avoids him at the event, when she leaves, he and his associate suddenly appear outside. Gary asks Alex to help him get his inebriated friend into the car. As she assists him in, she realizes she is being forced inside, and both men ignore her when she says she can find her own ride home. Instead, she quickly discovers they tricked her, and she is trapped. Shortly after the driver takes off, they hold her down and try to rape her. The only way she is spared is because as she tries to fight off the men, the driver hears the commotion, stops the car, and turns on the light. Alex rushes out of the car and begins to run away while Gary exclaims, "Let her go. She won't talk."[126]

After the attempted sexual assault, Alex experiences intense anxiety and fear. According to Claudia Avina and William O'Donahue, victims of sexual harassment and attempted assault like Alex tend to suffer from PTSD (Post Traumatic Stress Disorder).[127] Specific symptoms may include

123 Catherine A. MacKinnon, et al., *What's Next: Harnessing the #MeToo Movement and #TimesUp,* YouTube, Milken Institute (July 9, 2018), https://www.youtube.com/watch?v=Mv8Gd-WVvNwM

124 *Id.*

125 Katz, at 195.

126 Katz, at 341.

127 Claudia Avina and William O'Donahue, *Sexual Harassment and PTSD: Is Sexual Harassment Diagnosable Trauma?* Journal of Traumatic Stress, June 30, 2005, at 69, 69.

"re-experiencing, effortful avoidance, emotional numbing, and hyperarousal factors."[128] Having already experienced some of these symptoms after Gary gropes her, Alex stays home from work for a few days after the attempted rape. During this time, she suffers from re-experiencing the incident. She does not want to shower because "being naked made the whole night rush in on me, the pulsing music in my ears, the anxiety in my veins … I mostly heard my own screams, my own struggle. My body did not feel like my own any longer."[129] Although she had previously been experimenting with drugs and alcohol, one new hyperarousal symptom she experiences after returning to work includes additional "risky or destructive behaviors."[130] Specifically, in addition to taking other illegal drugs, Alex begins to take Xanax to calm her nerves. Along with using the drugs to numb herself emotionally, she tries to force herself to "snap out of it" because "nothing even happened."[131] She also uses her work as a means to disassociate: "Throwing myself into work distracted me from the mess that was my personal life, sucking all the emotion out of me and leaving behind a calculating shell of a human."[132] With these recognizable symptoms, the audience witnesses how quickly a young, smart, capable young woman devolves into an emotional and mental crisis. This shocking deterioration occurs in only a few months after working in a toxic environment that permits the grooming and sexual harassment of women.

Institutional Betrayal and DARVO in *The Boys Club*

When victims like Alex are not supported by the institution that is supposed to protect her and offer her safe working conditions, institutional betrayal occurs. As previously mentioned in the beginning of this chapter, institutional betrayal harms those who are dependent on the institution, and it happens "when an institution fails to prevent or respond supportively to wrongdoings … [and] there is a reasonable expectation of protection."[133] In previous chapters, I discussed a blame-shifting technique that perpetrators use against

128 Patrick A. Palmieri and Louise F. Fitzgerald, *Confirmatory Factor Analysis of Post-Traumatic Stress Symptoms in Sexually Harassed Women*, Journal of Traumatic Stress, Dec. 28 2005, 657, 657.

129 Katz, at 348.

130 NeuRA Libraries, *Hyperarousal: What are the Hyperarousal Symptoms of PTSD?*, NeuRA: Discover, Conquer, Cure (Oct. 7, 2021), https://library.neura.edu.au/ptsd-library/signs-and-symptoms-ptsd-library/general-signs-and-symptoms-signs-and-symptoms-ptsd-library/hyperarousal/index.html#:~:text=Hyperarousal%20is%20a%20core%20symptom,difficulty%20concentrating%2C%20and%20difficulty%20sleeping.

131 Katz, at 357.

132 *Id.* at 348.

133 Jennifer J. Freyd, *Institutional Betrayal*, Institutional Betrayal and Institutional Courage (Feb. 2023), https://dynamic.uoregon.edu/jjf/institutionalbetrayal/

victims of gendered violence: DARVO (Deny, Attack, Reverse Victim and Offender). On a larger scale, institutional DARVO arises when the institution dismisses both the harm to the victim and the wrongdoing of the perpetrator. As a result, these perpetrators may continue their abuse, and this leads to institutional betrayal that can "exacerbate the impact of traumatic experiences."[134] Specifically, victims who go through institutional betrayal may be subject to higher rates of PTSD, depression, and anxiety due to the violation of trust between the victim and the abuser and the victim and the institution.[135] In short, the victim is not only traumatized by the individual perpetrator but also by the institution that allows the abuse. At the end of the novel, Alex goes up against Klasko & Fitch's institutional betrayal and surprisingly wins. The audience discovers that Alex had used digital voice mail to record Gary's attempted sexual assault. She utilizes the recording on her phone as leverage to end sexual harassment at Klasko & Fitch and to create a "Women's Initiative Budget."[136] Although *The Boys Club* provides a happy ending, this type of ending is not a realistic one. Sexual harassment continues to pervade the workplace, and victims rarely have any institutional or legal recourse.

Conclusion

Sexual harassment is a unique form of violence against women. Unlike sexual assault, domestic violence, or stalking, sexual harassment is not a crime. However, successfully suing an employer for sexual harassment is an extremely difficult task and a rare occurrence. The law tends to side with the employer's antidiscrimination policies and practices that are in place—which do not favor the victim. As the *The Boys Club* demonstrates, when corporate leadership permits behavior such as discrimination and sexual harassment, this creates a culture of complicity. As a result, some higher-ranking men may prey upon lower-ranking women, and this may begin with grooming. In this instance, predators target young, less experienced women with psychoemotional vulnerabilities. These predators utilize their charm, power, and good looks to manipulate these women into having affairs with them. While some might argue that these affairs are "consensual," this is not the case. This is sexual harassment because there is a power differential between the two parties. In *The Boys Club*, Alex describes this type of sexual harassment as having sex with a "man [the woman] at best had feelings for and at worst was too worried to reject."[137] Another type of sexual harassment occurs when women

134 Carly Parnitzke Smith and Jennifer J. Freyd, *Dangerous Safe Havens: Institutional Betrayal Exacerbates Sexual Trauma*, in JOURNAL OF TRAUMATIC STRESS, 119, 119, 26.1 (2013).

135 JENNIFER J. FREYD AND PAMELA J. BIRRELL, BLIND TO BETRAYAL 1 (2013).

136 KATZ, at 387.

137 *Id.* at 324.

such as Alex are subjected to a variety of unwanted behaviors—from sexist slurs and comments to groping to attempted sexual assault. When victims are not supported by their supervisors, institutional betrayal and institutional DARVO arises. This can lead to the victim suffering from severe PTSD since she is betrayed both by the predator(s) and the institution that is supposed to protect her. In this chapter, I argue that, like sexual assault, domestic violence, and stalking, sexual harassment of women has most often been permitted due to longstanding gender roles that reinforce toxic masculinity and excuse violence.

6 Conclusion

Putting Theory Into Practice

For centuries, women have been disproportionately impacted by forms of gender-based violence. This concept is one that has crossed time periods, geographical locations, cultures, and contexts. It relies on outdated sexist stereotypes and biased social constructions that reinforce the superiority of males over females. Due to the nuances of both acquaintance crimes and gender biases, many forms of violence against women are most often ignored.[1] This challenge arises because both the law and a culture of disbelief of women require an irrational black and white explanation in a world full of gray areas. In this sense, victims are not only disregarded but are also often unfairly blamed for the perpetrator's abuse toward them. Although I do not have all the solutions, and there is still much work to be done, here are a few ideas I have gathered:

1. We, as a society, should begin by believing victims instead of the perpetrators. We should give survivors the benefit of the doubt when they claim they have been raped, domestically abused, stalked, or sexually harassed. From the beginning, survivors should be supported until and if the circumstances prove otherwise.
2. Legislators should listen to survivors and incorporate laws that better serve them. Legislators also need to understand that acquaintance crimes are unique due to the complex, personalized nature of the abuse.
3. Prosecutors should develop "collaborative, interdisciplinary response teams to address the complex social, economic, and psychological issues" present in violent crimes against women.[2] These teams can serve to help better educate not only prosecutors and legal personnel but also investigators, judges, and juries. For jury trials, prosecutors should use

1 Christine Chinkin, *Violence Against Women: The International Legal Response*, 3.2 GENDER AND DEVELOPMENT, 23, 23 (June 1995).

2 MICHELLE KAMINSKY, REFLECTIONS OF A DOMESTIC VIOLENCE PROSECUTOR: SUGGESTIONS FOR REFORM 15 (2012).

DOI: 10.4324/9781003303572-6

the *voir dire* process as an opportunity to train jurors on the subtleties of interpersonal violence and biases against victims.

4. Police officers should be provided with better training that focuses on the PTSD experienced by the victim, her response to abuse, and the complex nuances of acquaintance crimes.
5. If possible, judges for domestic violence, sexual assault, and stalking cases should be screened and selected by committees composed of experts who specialize in these areas. The committees should consist of participants from the criminal justice and family court systems and experts from the nonprofit sector.[3]
6. In sexual assault cases, each state should broaden its definition of a victim's nonconsent to include "disassociation" or "passivity and acquiescence."[4] This inclusion negates the impractical "fight" or "flight" binary and permits the more realistic "freeze" response. Since acquaintance rapes are rarely prosecuted, the law should do a better job of recognizing that the absence of resistance does not correlate to a victim's consent. On the contrary, only hearing or seeing someone say "yes" should represent their consent, and if someone is not actively participating, then they are not consenting to having sex. As such, consent may be withdrawn at any time.
7. As I mention in my stalking chapter, the crime of stalking is rarely prosecuted because prosecutors must prove a pattern of conduct instead of just one isolated incident. However, since stalking behaviors tend to be bold and undisguised, one solution for proving an incident could be to place more focus on the perpetrator's conduct instead of his intent to harass a victim "knowingly or willingly."[5]
8. Since the criminal justice system continues to struggle to assist domestic violence victims, states should create a domestic violence database for repeat offenders.[6] This database offers "a preventive—rather than remedial—approach to combating this pervasive social problem."[7] Similar to a sex offender database, this one should contain contact information of any perpetrator who acquires three domestic violence convictions.[8] In addition, harsher penalties should be enforced in states that allow for the possession of firearms. Specifically, guns should be taken away from

3 *Id.* at 16.

4 Catherine A. MacKinnon, *Rape Redefined*, Harvard Law and Policy Review 447 (June 14, 2016).

5 U.S. Dept. of Justice, Bureau of Justice Assistance, *Regional Seminar Series on Developing and Implementing Anti-Stalking Codes,* NCJ-156836 (June 1996).

6 J.Y. Young, *Three Strikes and You're In: Why the States Need Domestic Violence Databases*, 90 Tex. L. Rev. 771, 771 (2011-2012).

7 *Id.*

8 *Id.*

convicted domestic abusers who own them, and they should not be able to possess firearms under any circumstances.

9. As I mention in my domestic violence chapter, states should broaden the definition of "family violence" to include other forms of violence aside from physical abuse, threat of physical abuse, or harassment. Some examples that should be added include financial control, isolation, psychological abuse, and other types of coercive control.
10. Movies and television series are powerful forms of entertainment that contribute to viewers' understanding of gender roles.[9] As a result, this type of media should stop perpetuating sexist, inaccurate stereotypes of both women and men. For example, earlier Disney movies lend to the false notion that women are weak and helpless and need to be "saved" by men. Many movies and series with romantic themes instill a similar idea in addition to the notion that love is painful, and partners typically verbally and emotionally abuse one another through arguments, name-calling, lies, accusations, and cheating. While in reality, all humans make mistakes, these subjects help standardize the concept of toxic love. They also continue to normalize harmful gender norms and help to "create a climate conducive to violence against women."[10]
11. Educators and parents play a critical role in "addressing misogynistic beliefs and behaviors," and they can help challenge "socially constructed attitudes about gender."[11] Parents should stop reinforcing traditional gender norms that subjugate women. Children should be formally educated about gender equality "with a continuing curriculum running from kindergarten to twelfth grade."[12] Colleges and universities should incorporate permanent anti-gender-violence programs and require annual training for all members of the campus community. These programs should educate college students not only on subjects such as sexual assault, dating violence, harassment, and stalking but also on topics such as consent, DARVO (Deny, Attack, Reverse Victim and Offender), healthy relationships, and bystander awareness.
12. Religious organizations that promote male superiority and/or racial supremacy should reconsider these teachings. They need to understand that these biases not only reinforce spiritual abuse but also violence against women and the abuse of children. One solution is to include programs such as the ManKINDness Project that target boys and young

9 David Gauntlett, Media, Gender, and Identity: An Introduction, 3 (2nd ed. 2008)
10 Kaminsky, at 16.
11 *Id.*
12 *Id.*

men.[13] An interactive learning experience, the ManKINDness awareness project "ignite(s) candid dialogue about masculinity and challenge(s) the status quo on how boys and men learn to view girls and women."[14]

13. In my sexual harassment chapter, I cover some ways in which corporate and business leadership can do a better job at combating sexual harassment in the workplace. To begin, the law should require employers to create stricter anti-sexual-harassment policies.[15] However, since the laws currently rely on a company's policy, and since these policies tend to neglect victims and enable harassers, institutional leadership should do more to create standards that remove complicity in the workplace.[16] In addition to incorporating stricter rules, leaders must rigorously enforce those rules. Leaders should not placate a harasser and dismiss wrongdoing due to a harasser's history or contributions to the institution. They must support victims and terminate the abusers. Furthermore, corporate and business leadership should create educational programs and policies against adult grooming in the workplace.
14. To expand from the cis-gender, heterosexual male/female binary, legislators should create more inclusive gender-neutral statutes and "remove the reference to gender or sexuality of partners."[17]
15. Thanks to the #MeToo movement, we have moved a bit closer toward something that looks like equality. Nonetheless, many of those in power continue to reinforce the destructive gender norms that have normalized violence. These countervailing sources against progress and change are enormous, powerful, and sometimes silent. These sources are fearful that their power will be taken away from them. As a result, we, as a society need more male leaders to support and speak out against violence towards women since "it is not a women's issue." On the contrary, "it is a men's issue" because most abusers of women are men.[18] As actress Meryl Streep puts it, "Progress will happen when men take a stand. It's the chivalry of the 21st century."[19]

13 New Friends New Life, *The ManKINDness Project: An Awareness Curriculum for Teen Boys,* (2018), https://www.newfriendsnewlife.org/mankindness

14 *Id.*

15 *Id.*

16 Louise F. Fitzgerald, *Sexual Harassment: Violence Against Women in the Workplace,* 48.10 AMERICAN PSYCHOLOGIST 1010, 1073 (October 1993).

17 Caroline Morin, *Re-Traumatized: How Gendered Laws Exacerbate the Harm for Same-Sex Victims of Intimate Partner Violence*, in DOMESTIC VIOLENCE LAW 180, 180 (Nancy K.D. Lemon, ed., 2018).

18 JACKSON KATZ, *Violence Against Women—It's a Men's Issue*, TEDx (Nov. 2012), https://www.ted.com/talks/jackson_katz_violence_against_women_it_s_a_men_s_issue? language=en.

19 Aisha Harris, *"This Changes Everything" Review: Hollywood's Men Called to Action,* THE NEW YORK TIMES (Aug. 8, 2019), https://www.nytimes.com/2019/08/08/movies/this-changes-everything-review.html

16. Women should continue to fight for their own autonomy, independence, and equality. To that end, women should support all women, regardless of marital status, career position, or lifestyle choice. Since financial abuse is the main way in which perpetrators control victims of domestic violence, women with male partners or husbands should strive to maintain their own financial freedom.
17. Historically, females have been "cast in the supporting actress role to men," and this should change.[20] We need to continue to work hard to "reframe the narrative and re cast ourselves as the lead actor of our own lives."[21] We must keep fighting not only for ourselves and for our own equality but also for everyone else who belongs to a marginalized group. Ultimately, what is good for women is good for all of us.

20 *From Single at 30 to Unstoppable at 60: Love Lessons You Wish You Knew Sooner With Cindy Trimm, Women of Impact* (Jan. 24, 2024) (downloaded using ITunes).

21 *Id.*

Index